MW01717121

THE COMPACT BIBLE DICTIONARY

The Compact Bible Dictionary

Peter Toon
Fr. Herb Schneider, S.J.

SERVANT BOOKS
Ann Arbor, Michigan

Cover design and photographs by Michael P. Andaloro

Published by Servant Books
P.O. Box 8617
Ann Arbor, Michigan 48107

Printed in the United States of America
ISBN 0-89283-321-1

87 88 89 90 91 10 9 8 7 6 5 4 3 2 1

Contents

Introduction

ONE OF THE SIGNS of God's presence with us and work among us is the growing number of people who are sincerely and seriously reading the sacred Scriptures of the Old and New Testaments. As we read, we discover that although the Bible is made up of two Testaments and many books, it is a marvelous unity. Written by a variety of people over ten or more centuries and including history, poetry, letters, treatises, and prophetic oracles, it is nevertheless truly one Book. What unites all the individual books is that they all point, directly or indirectly to the Lord, Yahweh, whom we confess to be Father, Son, and Holy Spirit. In fact, we believe that the Holy Spirit guided and inspired the various authors and editors of the books to produce what has been and remains for the church of God a faithful record of God's revelation of himself, his will and purposes to mankind.

Thus the Bible is a book that can be read at various levels. It can be read as a collection of ancient documents giving insight into how people long ago practiced their religion and formed their beliefs. It can be read as literature to be enjoyed for its good stories and ethical insights. It can also be read—and this is how Christians particularly read it—as God's written Word: the Old Testament preparing the way for the Word made flesh, Jesus the Christ, and the New Testament describing his appearance, impact, and mission. Seen as the written Word of God because witnessing to and testifying of the eternal Word of God (the eternal Son), the Bible becomes a book not merely to be studied carefully but also is to be meditated upon prayerfully. Studying the text carefully must go hand in hand with meditating upon it prayerfully in the general context of faithful membership of the church and attendance at her services of worship, in order to use the Bible aright and to gain all that it has to offer us.

The purpose of Bible dictionaries, encyclopedias, lexicons, and concordances is to help us understand the text of Scripture. However, these sources also include information on the historical, geographical, economic, and cultural context of the books as well as the themes and teachings of individual books or of groups of books found in the two Testaments. Because we are separated from the original authors and editors of the books by many centuries, we need help to discover as quickly, efficiently, and accurately as possible what really they were seeking to convey to their own readers.

Obviously great help can be gained from the large and scholarly volumes used by theological students and clergy. Many of us, however, cannot find time to use such books, even if we felt confident enough to try to do so. We read the Bible when we have time—traveling to work, in the lunch break, or waiting for a meal. To help us understand what we read, we often find that we need instant help—usually minimal help—in order to benefit as fully as possible from our reading. Such help may be, for example, to identify the Pharisees or to discover the names of the kings of Judah or Israel.

So to accompany our Bible we need a compact dictionary. We expect from this handbook the basic information needed to help us read the Bible with understanding and thus enabling us to meditate upon its message fruitfully and to put its teaching into practice in our daily lives. The *Compact Bible Dictionary* is designed to meet this need.

How to Use It

Begin by looking in the *Index* for the topic on which you want information. Then read the appropriate entries and follow up by reading the Scripture references at the end of each brief entry. These are meant to enlarge the understanding already gained by digesting the contents of the entries. If you want to meditate upon one or another of the themes of sacred Scripture and seek to obey our Lord each day, you will find that this *Compact Bible Dictionary* is excellent.

List of Abbreviations

Books of the Old Testament

Genesis	Gn
Exodus	Ex
Leviticus	Lv
Numbers	Nm
Deuteronomy	Dt
Joshua	Jos
Judges	Jgs
Ruth	Ru
1 Samuel	1 Sm
2 Samuel	2 Sm
1 Kings	1 Kgs
2 Kings	2 Kgs
1 Chronicles	1 Chr
2 Chronicles	2 Chr
Ezra	Ezr
Nehemiah	Neh
Tobit	Tb
Judith	Jdt
Esther	Est
Job	Jb
Psalms	Ps
Proverbs	Prv
Ecclesiastes	Eccl
Song of Songs	Sg
Wisdom	Wis
Sirach	Sir
Isaiah	Is
Jeremiah	Jer
Lamentations	Lam
Baruch	Bar
Ezekiel	Ez
Daniel	Dn
Hosea	Hos
Joel	Jl
Amos	Am
Obadiah	Ob
Jonah	Jon
Micah	Mi
Nahum	Na
Habakkuk	Hb
Zephaniah	Zep
Haggai	Hg
Zechariah	Zec
Malachi	Mal
1 Maccabees	1 Mc
2 Maccabees	2 Mc

Books of the New Testament

Matthew	Mt
Mark	Mk
Luke	Lk
John	Jn
Acts of the Apostles	Acts
Romans	Rom
1 Timothy	1 Tm
2 Timothy	2 Tm
Titus	Ti
Philemon	Phlm
Hebrews	Heb
James	Jas

1 Corinthians	1 Cor
2 Corinthians	2 Cor
Galatians	Gal
Ephesians	Eph
Philippians	Phil
Colossians	Col
1 Thessalonians	1 Thes
2 Thessalonians	2 Thes
1 Peter	1 Pt
2 Peter	2 Pt
1 John	1 Jn
2 John	2 Jn
3 John	3 Jn
Jude	Jude
Revelation	Rv

ONE

Books of the Bible and Related Literature

Acts of the Apostles. The second half of the story of which the Gospel of Luke is the first. The "acts" may be seen as the apostolic ministries of (mainly) Peter and Paul or as the operations of the Holy Spirit through committed disciples of Jesus. The book covers the first thirty years of Christianity from the Ascension of Jesus and the descent of the Spirit at Pentecost. Beginning in Jerusalem (ch. 1-7), the movement spread into Judea and Samaria (8-12) and throughout the northern Mediterranean world (13-28). Originally composed only of Jews, it became a people from both Jewish and non-Jewish (Gentile) backgrounds—a truly international society.
See also **Luke, Gospel of,** sec. 1.

Amos, Book of. An anthology of the oracles of the prophet Amos, who was a shepherd from Tekoa, in the southern kingdom of Judah. They date from the reign of Jeroboam II (c. 786-c. 746 B.C.), a period of prosperity and corruption for the northern kingdom of Israel and its capital, Samaria. The first section (1:1-2:5) contains messages of divine judgment upon Israel's neighbors for their crimes against humanity. In the second (2:6-6:14) are messages to Israel of judgment and woe because of its failure to keep God's covenant in terms of both duty to God and to mankind. The final section (7-9)

contains five symbolic visions of divine threats and promises concerning Israel's future.
See also **Amos,** sec. 2.

Apocalyptic Literature (Gk., *apocalypsis,* "unveiling, revelation"). Whole books or parts of books within the Bible or Jewish and Christian literature (c. 200 B.C.-A.D.150). In them imagery, metaphor, and symbolism (often bizarre) are used to communicate secrets concerning such themes as God's intervention in history, the end of the world, and the future of the wicked and the righteous. For the OT see Is 24-27, 56-66; Joel; Zec 9-14; and Daniel; for the NT see Mt 24; Mk 13; Lk 21; 1 Thes 4:16-17; 2 Thes 2, and Revelation.

Apocrypha (Gk., "hidden books"). As used by Protestants, it refers to those books, or parts of books, which were reckoned as OT by the early church (and by the Council of Trent, 1546) but are not in the Hebrew Bible. Jerome called them "apocrypha," but the practice of collecting them into a separate unit dates back no further than A.D. 1520. The fifteen books, or parts of books, are: Tobit; Judith; part of the book of Esther; Wisdom of Solomon; Ecclesiasticus (Sirach); Baruch; the Letter of Jeremiah; the Song of the Three; Daniel and Susanna; Daniel, Bel, and the Dragon; and the First and Second Books of the Maccabees.
See also **Canon,** sec. 1.

Apocrypha (NT). Writings from after A.D. 100 that resemble books within the NT. There are (1) *apocryphal Gospels,* claiming to provide extra details about Jesus, e.g., *Gospel of the Nazarenes* and *Gospel of the Hebrews;* (2) *apocryphal Acts,* recounting the travels and miracles of the apostles, e.g., Acts of John, Paul, Peter, and Thomas; (3) *apocryphal Epistles,* developing privileges of certain churches or contents of doctrines, e.g., *Third Epistle to the Corinthians* and *Epistle to the Laodiceans;* and (4) *apocalypses* concerning the future, e.g., of Peter, Paul, Thomas, Stephen, and John.

Apocrypha (OT). Writings from c. 200 B.C.-A.D. 200 resembling books within the OT. Protestants prefer to call them *Pseudepigrapha.* The books are of two basic types: of either a Palestinian or a Hellenistic origin. Examples from the Palestinian context are the *Assumption of Moses* and the *Book of Enoch* (both cited in the NT in Jude); and from the Hellenistic context (Jewish communities outside Palestine) are *Third* and *Fourth Maccabees* and the *Sibylline Oracles.*

Aramaic. The language most widely spoken in Palestine in the time of Jesus. It is a close cognate rather than a derivative of Hebrew. Parts of the OT are in Aramaic: Dn 2:4-7:28; Ezr 4:8-6:18, 7:12-26; Jer 10:11. Targums are Aramaic translations of parts of the Hebrew text of the Bible. In the NT a few Aramaic words or phrases appear: *talitha koum* (Mk 5:41), *ephphatha* (Mk 7:34), and *Maranatha* (1 Cor 16:22) See also **Hebrew,** sec. 1.

Baruch, Book of. A short OT book ascribed to Baruch, the secretary of Jeremiah the prophet. Beginning with a prayer of penitence (1:1-3:8) it continues with a poem celebrating the wisdom in the Law of Moses (3:9-4:4) and with songs of comfort (4:5-5:9). It ends with the Letter of Jeremiah (6:1-73), an attack on idolatry in the form of a letter to the Jewish exiles in Babylon.

This book is not in the Hebrew canon and thus not in Protestant Bibles.

See **Baruch,** sec. 2.

Canon (Gk., "rule"). Since the fourth century, "canon" has denoted an authoritative list of books, inspired by God and belonging to the OT and NT. The Jewish canon, listing only Hebrew books, is shorter than the OT canon accepted by the Catholic church, because in the latter books extant only in Greek are counted as OT. These are known as deutero-canonical writings (secondary canon). Protestants call these extra books the Apocrypha and do not include them in the OT.

The canon of the NT began to take formal shape around A.D. 200, due primarily to the challenge to orthodoxy from heretical teaching. For over a century the Gospels, Acts, and Epistles had been circulating among the churches. The canon reached its final shape of twenty-seven books in the fourth century: in the East in the Thirty-ninth Paschal Letter of Athanasius (367), and in the West by the Council of Carthage in 397.

Catholic Epistles. The Letters of James, Peter (2), John (3), and Jude are so called because they were addressed to a wider group than one local church congregation.

Chronicles, First and Second Books of. These tell the story of Israel from the beginning of the monarchy under Saul to the return from exile in Babylon, a period of five centuries. The contents fall into four parts. (1) Genealogical tables (1 Chr 1-9) tracing the line of descent from Adam to those who returned from Exile; (2) the acts of David (1 Chr 10-29); (3) the acts of Solomon (2 Chr 1-9); and (4) the history of Judah from the rebellion of the northern tribes to the Exile (2 Chr 10-36). The story is continued in the book of Ezra.

In the choice and treatment of material, these books have specific emphases: concern for and commitment to faithful worship; Judah as the leader of the twelve tribes; and the need for trusting obedience of God. Thus these books are not inferior to 1 and 2 Samuel and 1 and 2 Kings, but take a different approach to history. They are less political and more ecclesiastical or theological in tone. The date of their composition is uncertain, probably between 537 and 331 B.C.

Colossians, Epistle of Paul to the. Although he had not founded the church in Colossae, Paul had heard of it from Epaphras. While there was much in its life and witness for which to thank God, there was also cause for concern because of false teaching. The latter came in the form of a fusion of Christian teaching with Gnosticism (of a Jewish variety). So from his house arrest in Rome in A.D. 60-61 the apostle addressed the church. He insisted that Jesus Christ is the Creator and Lord and thus above all powers or spirits in the universe; in him is revealed God's true wisdom, and the way of holiness is not via false asceticism and outward observances in matters of food and drink but by essential union with Jesus in his death, resurrection, and exaltation. See **Colossae,** sec. 3.

Corinthians, First and Second Epistles of Paul to the. Having founded the church in the cosmopolitan city of Corinth, he wrote his first letter after he had met a delegation from it in Ephesus in A.D. 54. They reported urgent problems needing solution. He took up four matters: divisions within the congregation, court cases between members, misuse and abuse of Christian freedom, and lack of discipline in some services of worship. Further he responded to five questions from the church: on marriage and celibacy, on food that came from sacrifices offered to idols, on the place of women in the congregation, on spiritual gifts, and on the resurrection of the body. Chapter 13, a celebration of love, is one of the great chapters of the Bible.

A year or two later Paul wrote what is called the Second Epistle. However, before writing it he made a short, "painful" visit and wrote a letter in anguish to the church. This lost letter had a positive effect and when Paul received this news he wrote 2 Corinthians. Its intensely personal character with recurring themes makes it difficult to analyze. It provides, however, tremendous insight into Paul's ministry, suffering, faith, and care for the churches.
See **Corinth,** sec. 3.

Daniel, Book of. This OT book of prophecy falls into two parts. Chapters 1-6 are basically historical in content: the writer, Daniel, speaking in the third person. He is taken from his homeland, Judah, to Babylon. Here he is seen serving various kings and interpreting their dreams. In chapters 7-12 Daniel speaks in the first person as he receives from God dreams whose content relates to the destiny of Israel in the context of the heathen Gentile kingdoms.

Modern critical scholarship is nearly unanimous in its rejection of the traditional view that the book was actually composed by Daniel. Instead of a sixth-century date, it is claimed that the work was composed during the persecution of Jews by Antiochus Epiphanes (167-164 B.C.) by an unknown author who used Daniel's name to give his message of comfort an added authority.

The episodes of Susanna and of Bel and the Dragon (ch. 13-14) are found only in the Greek version of Daniel, and thus are classified as apocrypha in Protestant Bibles.
See **Daniel,** sec. 2.

Dead Sea Scrolls. The popular name given to manuscripts found in caves west of the Dead Sea since 1947. They belonged to a religious community of Jews at Qumran and were hidden in A.D. 68 when the Roman army moved against rebel Jews. Written in both Aramaic and Hebrew, they provide important information about Jewish religious life in the period of Jesus and the birth of the church. They also give important insights into the transmission of the text of the OT.

Deuteronomy, Book of (Gk., "second law"). The fifth book of Moses and thus the last of the Pentateuch. It is called a "second law" because it contains a fresh statement of the laws God previously gave at Mount Sinai (recorded in Ex, Lv, and Nm): here they are applied to the forthcoming settled life in Canaan as Moses gives his farewell addresses to Israel on the plains of Moab, on the eve of entry into the promised land. The book falls into three sections: (1) 1:1-4:43, Moses' first address; (2) 4:44-28:68, his second address; (3) 29:1-30:20, his third address; and (4) the last acts of Moses before his death.

Traditionally it has been assumed that Moses is the effective author of this book; but modern scholarship, while accepting that much of the material goes back to Moses, argues that it was composed several centuries after the Israelites had been settled in Canaan. Jesus quoted from this book in his testing by Satan in the wilderness (Mt 3).
See also **Pentateuch,** sec. 1.

Ecclesiastes, Book of. This title is the Greek translation of *Qoheleth,* the Hebrew for "preacher" or "teacher" and points to the author's official title rather than to his name. It presents a popular form of religious writing in near eastern countries in OT times. Reflections on life from a variety of angles are given in prose and in verse aphorisms. It takes its place in the Bible because the author teaches that only by faith in God can one gain the key to human life. Without God its enigma cannot be solved, but with him life can have true joy and satisfaction. Thus the last word of the book is: "Fear God and keep his commandments, for this is man's all."
The identity of the author is unknown. If king Solomon was the original writer, its language was later modernized, for it reflects c. 200 B.C.
See **Wisdom Literature,** sec. 1.

Ephesians, Epistle of Paul to the. It would appear that this letter, written by Paul from prison in Rome (A.D. 61-63), was intended as a circular letter to a group of churches, including Ephesus. The reason for this view is that it contains no personal greetings and has no reference to specific problems or joys in the church of Ephesus: then, also, the words "at Ephesus" (1:1) are missing in some early Greek manuscripts.
It contains a rich and high theology of the marvelous eternal purpose of God in Jesus Christ, followed by an urgent exhortation to live worthily in the light and strength of the high calling of God in Christ Jesus.
See **Ephesus,** sec. 3.

Epistle, Letter. In the NT, twenty-one books are called epistles or letters; they display a variety of literary forms.

There are thirteen under Paul's name, one anonymous "To the Hebrews," two under Peter's name, three under John's, and one under Jude's. All were written in the second half of the first century and represent the only source for knowledge of what the apostles believed, taught, and confessed.

The most personal is Paul's Letter to Philemon and the most artistic and literary is the Letter to the Hebrews. Of Paul's letters the first to be written were those to Galatia and Thessalonica, around A.D. 50. Ephesians, Colossians, Philemon, and Philippians are called Prison Letters (Captivity Epistles) because all were written from prison in Ephesus or Rome. The Pastoral Epistles are 1 and 2 Timothy and Titus. The terms General Letters or Catholic Epistles are used of 1 and 2 Peter; 1, 2, and 3 John; James; and Jude.

Esther, Book of. Named after its Jewish heroine, Esther, queen of the Persian king, Xerxes (Ahasuerus). It tells the story of how she was able to save the Jewish community from massacre. Further, it explains the origin of the feast of Purim.

In Jewish tradition Mordecai, Esther's adoptive father, is regarded as the author of the original Hebrew text: the latter does not use the name of God but contains a doctrine of divine providence. The longer Greek text, with an extra 107 verses, does use God's name: it dates from c. 114 B.C.
See **Esther,** sec. 2, and **Feasts,** sec. 4.

Exodus, Book of (Gk., *exodos,* "going out"). The second Book of Moses in the Pentateuch. It records the deliverance of Israel from Egypt and the giving of the Law. The contents are: (1) the Israelites in Egypt, an oppressed people (1:1-12:36); (2) deliverance from Egypt and journey to Mount Sinai (12:37-18:27); (3) making of the Covenant between God and Israel (19:1-24:18); and (4) the Tabernacle, God's dwelling, and its furnishings (25:1-40:38).
See **Pentateuch,** sec. 1.

Ezekiel, Book of. The prophecies are arranged in roughly chronological order and dated according to the year of king

Jehoiachin's captivity by the Babylonians (from 597 to at least 562 B.C.). The prophet himself was also taken as captive into Babylon and there he prophesied. The oracles are in three divisions: (1) those delivered before the capture of Jerusalem, foretelling its overthrow (1-24); (2) those addressed to various nations, announcing the divine judgment (25-32); (3) those promising restoration of Israel, its land, and its Temple (33-48). Throughout the book there is a majestic doctrine of God who has zeal for his own holy name.
See **Ezekiel,** sec. 2.

Ezra, Book of. The continuation of the narrative of 1 and 2 Chronicles, providing an account of the return of Jews from Exile between 538 and 433 B.C. In chapters 1-6 there is a narrative of the return under Sheshbazzar in 538 with the restoration of divine service and the rebuilding of the Temple. Chapters 7-10 present the return of another group of exiles under Ezra in 458 and of his successful attempts to bring a halt to the intermarriage of Jews with foreigners.

In this book are copies of public records and official documents, written in Aramaic (the language of international commerce and diplomacy). In the Hebrew Bible, Ezra and Nehemiah are counted as one book. In composition, they belong to the same period as 1 and 2 Chronicles.

The Vulgate divides Ezra-Nehemiah, calling the former the First Book of Esdras and the latter the Second Book of Esdras.
See **Nehemiah, Book of,** sec. 1 and **Ezra,** sec. 2.

Galatians, Epistle of Paul to the. Written by the apostle with a great sense of urgency and passion to set aside the false teaching of the Judaizers. They had cast doubts on Paul's apostolic status and taught the necessity of conformity to minimal Judaism by Gentile Christians. In response, Paul sought to make clear the nature of salvation by the grace of God, arguing that for Gentiles this does not mean conformity to Judaism. The apostle's doctrine is stated in a larger format in his Epistle to the Romans.

Since "Galatia" was used of two areas in what is now Turkey (ethnic Galatia and the Roman province of Galatia) it is not absolutely clear to which area the letter originally went. If it was to the Roman province then it was to the churches of Pisidian Antioch, Iconium, Lystra, and Derbe (Acts 13:14-14:23) but if to ethnic Galatia, then to churches in the area mentioned in Acts 16:6 and 18:23.
See **Galatia,** sec. 3.

Genesis, the Book of (Gk., *genesis,* "beginning"). The book of beginnings—the first Book of Moses and of the Pentateuch, telling of the making of the universe, the creation of mankind, the origins of sin, and the election by God of a people. The contents may be divided as follows: (1) prehistory or primeval history (1:1-11:26); (2) Abraham (11:27-25:18); (3) Isaac and Jacob (25:19-36:43); and (4) Joseph and his brothers (37:1-50:26).

Though chapters 1-11 are not scientific history, they are very important for their symbolic presentation of important truths about God and his creation.
See **Pentateuch** and **Creation,** sec. 6.

Gospels. There is no biography of Jesus; the four Gospels, although containing biographical information and making use of authentic eyewitness testimony, are booklets of a unique literary genre. Their basic purpose is to present the good news from God concerning the life, teaching, death, and resurrection of Jesus, the Messiah. They are designed to encourage their readers to believe in Jesus and gain eternal life from God.

It was at least thirty years after the Ascension that the first Gospel, Mark's, appeared. Until that time, as well as after it, material concerning Jesus was carefully preserved in the churches and passed on both in written form and by word of mouth.

The first three Gospels (Mt, Mk, and Lk) have been called the Synoptic Gospels since 1774 because they lend themselves to study by their texts being placed in parallel columns to show coincidences.
See **Matthew, Mark, Luke,** and **John, Gospels of.**

Greek. The NT books are all in common Greek (*koine*), which was widely spoken in the Roman Empire. After the conquests of Alexander the Great, Greek came to be widely used, and this usage continued when the Roman replaced the Greek empire. By the time of the NT, Latin was beginning to make an impact on this Greek, especially on vocabulary, e.g., the word *kentyrion* (centurion). It is also possible to discern in the Greek of some NT books the influence of Hebrew or Aramaic, especially in the Revelation of John.

Habakkuk, Book of. The collection of prophecies usually dated shortly after the battle of Carchemish (605 B.C.). Here the Egyptians were defeated, allowing the Chaldeans to march east where eventually Nebuchadnezzar invaded Judah and captured Jerusalem (597 B.C.). Habakkuk, about whom virtually nothing is known, addressed himself to the moral problem of God causing a cruel and barbarous Chaldean army to be the means of his judgment upon his elect people (Jews) and their land (Judah). Chapters 1-2 consist of a dialogue between the prophet and God, while chapter 3 is a wonderful lyrical prayer, ending in joyful confidence in God.
See **Habakkuk,** sec. 2.

Haggai, Book of. Having returned from Exile, Haggai delivered these oracles between August and December, 520 B.C. They were delivered in Jerusalem at a time when the returned exiles were discouraged in their work of rebuilding God's house, the Temple, but yet were living in their own houses. They contain a message of encouragement and hope.
See **Haggai,** sec. 2

Hebrew. Member of the western group of Semitic languages. Abraham learned it when he settled in Canaan. Within the OT it is called the "language of Canaan" (Is 19:18) or the "language of Judah" (Is 36:11). It was spoken until the Exile (597 B.C.) but was then replaced as the vernacular by Aramaic. However, Hebrew has remained as the classical language of Scripture and of Judaism to this day. Jesus was familiar with it through the synagogue, but he spoke Aramaic in daily life. It is written from right to left.

Modern Hebrew, the language of the State of Israel, is derived from classical Hebrew.

Hebrews, Epistle to the. The author of this work, which is more like a short treatise or exhortation than a letter, is not known. He appears to have been a Greek-speaking Jewish Christian leader who wrote before A.D. 96 to fellow Jews—hence the title, "to the Hebrews." His readers were being pressured to return to Judaism and thus he sought to strengthen them in their faith in Jesus, the Messiah. He presented the Christianity of the new covenant as the completion and goal of the Judaism of the old covenant.

Written in a polished style, the letter presents the superiority of Christianity to all previous and possible revelation, unfolds the value and implications of Christ's unique high priesthood, and urges the readers to live by this superlative faith with a renewed confidence in Jesus, the same yesterday, today, and forever.

Hosea, Book of. Prophecies delivered in the northern kingdom of Israel over thirty years, from a point in the reign of Jeroboam II (786-746 B.C.) until just before the fall of the capital, Samaria, in 722 B.C. It was a period of apostasy, infidelity to God's covenant, oppression of the poor by the rich and powerful, and threat of invasion by Assyria.

Hosea portrayed Israel as an adulterous, faithless wife whom the Lord, because of his love for her, could not give up (1-3). In reality Israel had gone over to the worship of Baal, the Caananite deity. In chapters 4-14 Israel's guilt and

punishment is portrayed and the call is given. "Return, O Israel, to the Lord, your God" who is the God of love.
See **Hosea,** sec. 2, and **Baal**, sec. 4.

Isaiah, Book of. This long book falls into four sections. Chapters 1-35 contain oracles addressed to the people of Judah, 742-687 B.C.; 36-39 are a historical appendix, almost identical to 2 Kgs 18-20; 40-55, sometimes called Deutero-Isaiah, contain oracles which presuppose the exile in Babylon in the sixth century and foretell liberation and the restoration of Jerusalem; and 56-66, sometimes called Trito-Isaiah, contain a variety of oracles, some quite majestic.

Most scholars hold that the prophet Isaiah, whose call is in chapter 6, is responsible for virtually all of the oracles in 1-35; but, since chapters 40-55 presuppose the Exile, which occurred a century after Isaiah's time, they believe that another prophet, whose name is unknown, delivered these oracles from "the holy One of Israel." Chapters 56-66 are said to be either from the unknown prophet responsible for 40-55 or another anonymous prophet. In addition, chapters 24-27, known as the Apocalypse of Isaiah, are probably from a period later than the original prophet.

Jewish tradition considers one prophet the author of the whole book, including those parts assigned by modern scholarship to other anonymous prophets. It is indeed possible that God could have revealed the events, problems, and language of the future to an eighth-century prophet. Nevertheless, the hypothesis of at least two authors is convincing in view of the textual evidence and of the ancient habit of collecting related work from various periods under a well-known name.

Questions of authorship should not detract from the majestic quality of the contents of this book.
See **Isaiah,** sec. 2.

Jeremiah, Book of. These prophecies were delivered in Judah between 626 and 587 B.C. during the reign of five kings from Josiah to Zedekiah. They are in three sections: (1)

prediction of the approaching judgment on Judah and the promise of restoration after exile (2-33); (2) the execution of this judgment and the fall of Jerusalem (34-44); and (3) predictions concerning foreign nations (46-51).

The oracles are not presented in historical sequence, so the chapters may be arranged in terms of the five reigns: (1) Josiah, chapters 1-20 (except 12:7-13:27); (2) Jehoahaz—nothing; (3) Jehoiakim, chapters 26, 22-23, 25, 35-36, 45, 33, and 12:7-13:27; (4) Jehoiachin, chapters 13:18-19, 20:24-30, and 52:31-34; (5) Zedekiah, chapters 24, 29, 27-28, 51:59-60 and 30-33, 21, 34, 37-39. Chapters 40-44 were delivered after the fall of Jerusalem and 46-51 refer to other nations.

Jeremiah prophesied that God would make a new covenant with his people (24:7; 31:33-34; 32:39-40) and would send the Messiah (23:5-8; 30:4-11; 33:14-26).
See **Jeremiah,** sec. 2.

Job, Book of. One of the great works of poetry in the world. It cannot be placed exclusively in any one literary type, either epic, dramatic, didactic, or reflective. This said, it is usually classified as part of Jewish wisdom literature. It deals with the question, why does the righteous man suffer in a world whose judge is himself the holy and righteous Lord? Job, a prosperous and good man, loses possessions and family and catches a horrible disease. Why does such a thing happen in God's world? Job comes to see that God's ways can never be wholly understood or justified by mere mortals and he realizes that suffering is not always judgment from God, for it can be the chastisement of a loving Father.

Since it contains no definite historical clues, it cannot be precisely dated further, and its author is unknown.
See **Wisdom Literature,** sec. 1 and **Job,** sec. 2.

Joel, Book of. Four topics are covered in this short prophecy. (1) The devastation caused by plagues of locusts, pointing to divine judgment; (2) God's blessings on the land when the people repent; (3) the future outpouring of the Holy Spirit; and (4) final judgment upon the nations and salvation for God's elect. The oracle concerning the Holy Spirit was fulfilled on the day of Pentecost (Acts 2).

The date of the book could be as early as the eighth and as late as the fourth century B.C. All we know of Joel is that he was Pethuel's son.

See **Joel,** sec. 2

John, Gospel of. Written probably after the other three Gospels with the specific aim of bringing its readers to belief in Jesus as the Messiah and to receive through him eternal life from God. It is basically a sophisticated evangelistic booklet, whose aim is to present the words and deeds of Jesus in such a manner as to reveal his true identity—Son of God become Man.

The contents fall into three parts: (1) the revelation of Jesus, Son of God, to the world (1-12); (2) the revelation of Jesus to the disciples (13-17); and (3) the glorification of Jesus in death and resurrection (18-21).

As to authorship, the traditional view is that it was written by John the apostle, probably assisted by an amanuensis, about A.D. 90. Another suggestion is that it was written by a disciple of the apostle using the information gained from the apostle.

See **Gospels,** sec. 1 and **John,** sec. 2.

John, First, Second, and Third Epistles of. While the first is like a theological tract, the second and third are real letters. The style and content of the first is so like that of the Gospel of John that it must have the same author. It was written to combat false teaching concerning the identity of Jesus and the nature of sin against God; it shows how integrated are right doctrine and right conduct.

The other two letters are written by one who calls himself "the Elder," a title suggesting age, authority, and respect. Thus it is likely that they come from the apostle, one being addressed to a specific church and the other to an individual. See **John,** sec. 2.

Jonah, Book of. Prophecy in the form of a story. Chapter 1 tells how Jonah went in the opposite direction to God's call. He was thrown overboard in a storm. Chapter 2 gives the text of a prayer he offered from inside the belly of the great fish which swallowed him. Chapter 3 describes how, being disgorged by the fish on the shore, he went to Nineveh to preach God's message there. It may be taken as historical (history with a moral) or as a parable in historical form. Its theme is that God's love extends beyond Israel to the whole world.
See **Jonah,** sec. 2 and **Nineveh,** sec. 3.

Joshua, Book of. The story of the invasion (c. 1240 B.C.), conquest and division of the land of Canaan by the Israelites under Joshua, Moses' successor. It is the history of Israel from the death of Moses to that of Joshua, and it demonstrated God's faithfulness in giving to the descendants of Abraham, the land he had promised to him as an inheritance.

In the Hebrew Bible, this book is the first of the Former Prophets, which tell of Israel's history from the entry into Canaan to the Exile in Babylon. Scholars find this book impossible to date because of its many different editings.
See **Joshua,** sec. 2.

Jude, Epistle of. A brief letter written by Jude, a close relative of Jesus. It was addressed to a Christian community harrassed by false, arrogant teachers, advocating an exaggerated form of freedom. The elderly Jude urges the faithful to build upon the body of truth they have been given and to live as those who expect the return of Christ as judge.

In vv. 14-15 there is a quotation from the apocryphal Book of Enoch while the story in v. 9 comes from the apocryphal Assumption of Moses.
See **Apocrypha** (OT), sec. 1 and **Jude,** sec. 2.

Judges, Book of. The story of Israel's experience in Canaan from the death of Joshua to the rise of Samuel (c. 1220-1050 B.C.). Its title comes from the name of "judge" given to the twelve military leaders, who were inspired by God to save the Israelites from idolatry and external dangers. The narrative reveals the tendency towards sin present even in decent, religious people as it tells of the continuing cycle of desertion of the covenant, of God, and of his worship for the service of the local Canaanite deities. God's salvation is set forth in his response to the cry of his people when they reaped the fruit of their apostasy: he sent the "judges" to deliver them.

Judith, Book of. Not in the Hebrew Bible. The fictitious story, set in the reign of Nebuchadnezzar, of how a small Jewish town resisted the power of a heathen army because it was inspired by the example of a devout widow, Judith. It was probably written c. 150-125 B.C. at the time of the Maccabean revolt with the aim of strengthening the commitment of the Jewish people both to their God and to religious duties. The high points of the book are the speeches by Achior and the prayers and speeches of Judith. The beautiful hymn of the people blessing Judith (15:9-10) has often been applied to the Virgin Mary in the liturgy.

Kings, First and Second Books of. These two books continue the history provided by 1 and 2 Samuel. They form a continuous narrative covering four centuries of the history of Israel, from the close of David's reign to the fall of Samaria (722 B.C.) and Jerusalem (587 B.C.). Beginning with a stable, united kingdom, the story ends with destruction and deportation to Babylon. The contents are (1) the reign of Solomon (1 Kgs 1-11); (2) the divided kingdom (making Israel and Judah—1 Kgs 12-2 Kgs 17) and (3) the kingdom of Judah (2 Kgs 18-25).

The religious purpose of the books is to review the history leading up to the Exile in order to explain why divine judgment occurred, and to point to a better way for the future. The whole work was probably composed by a "prophetic writer" during the exile in Babylon; it makes use of various written sources ("the book of the acts of Solomon," 1 Kgs 11:41 and "the book of the chronicles of the kings of Israel," 1 Kgs 14:19).

Lamentations, Book of. The theme of the five elegies or mournful poems in this book is the capture and destruction of Jerusalem, with the terrible suffering of those events. Traditionally they are attributed to the prophet Jeremiah. The first, second, fourth, and fifth each have twenty-two verses, and each verse of 1, 3, and 4 begins with a different letter of the Hebrew alphabet (which has 22 letters); the fifth does not have an alphabetical arrangement. The third has sixty-six verses divided into twenty-two parts, each part starting with a different Hebrew letter. Thus 1-4 are acrostic. These poems are read in Jewish synagogues each July to recall the destruction of the Temple of Jerusalem in 587 B.C. and A.D. 70.

Leviticus, Book of. The third book of Moses in the Pentateuch. The title "relating to the Levites" derives from the Septuagint. Its theme is expressed in the words: "I, the Lord, am your God; you shall make and keep yourselves holy, because I am holy" (11:44; 19:2). God's holiness is his unique, majestic purity: however, that which is set apart for his worship and service is also called holy, in a derivative sense. The law, rules, and regulations of this book (given through divine revelation to Moses and Aaron) regulate access to God and so promote holiness at the human level. The narrative sections, continuing from the book of Exodus, relate Israel's experiences at Mount Sinai.
See **Levites,** sec. 4.

Luke, Gospel of. The first part of a two-part treatise (Luke-Acts) on the origins of the Christian faith, addressed to Theophilus, a Gentile Christian. It was written by Luke, a

physician and a friend and colleague of Paul (Col 4:14). He appears to have used about half of Mark's Gospel, together with other sources, to write this Gospel. He presents Jesus as the Christ for outsiders (i.e., non-Jews) and outcasts (Samaritans, tax collectors, prostitutes, etc.) as well as for insiders (Pharisees and ordinary Jews). Therefore Jesus is the universal Christ and as the Christ he was not only conceived by the Holy Spirit but filled with the Spirit to accomplish the work of the Messiah. Further, he was innocent of all political charges brought against him (a point that Gentiles needed to know) by his enemies.
See **Gospels, Acts,** sec. 1 and **Luke,** sec. 2.

Maccabees, First and Second Books of. Part of the OT for Roman Catholics but not in the Hebrew (Jewish) Bible and not regarded as Scripture by Protestants. They provide important information about and insight into the suppression of Judaism by the Greek Empire in the second century B.C.

First Maccabees was written about 100 B.C. and is a historical work of great value, providing an account of the Jewish war of independence under the Maccabee family of Levites. Written originally in Hebrew, it survived only in Greek translation. It begins with the accession of the Greek king, Antiochus IV (175 B.C.) and closes with the death of Simon Maccabee (134 B.C.).

Second Maccabees is not a sequel to 1 Maccabees and is by a different author. It covers events from 180-161 B.C. and provides a theological interpretation of them. In terms of the development of doctrine, the teaching on the resurrection of the righteous at the Last Day, the intercession of the saints in heaven for pilgrims on earth, and the power of the living to offer sacrifices and prayers for the dead are very important.
See **Maccabee,** sec. 2.

Malachi, Book of. The last book of the OT: it provides insights into the life of the Jewish community, recently

returned to Jerusalem from Exile. The oracles were delivered just before the arrival of Ezra (458 B.C.) but at a time when the new Temple was standing and sacrifices were being offered. Thus the prophecy belongs to the period after the work of the prophets Haggai and Zechariah. Malachi (Heb., "my messenger") rebuked the people in God's name for their failure to set and maintain high standards in worship and morality: further, he spoke of the coming great "day of the Lord."
See **Malachi,** sec. 2.

Mark, Gospel of. The shortest and earliest of the four Gospels, written between A.D. 64 and 70. It begins with the ministry of John the Baptist and concludes with the departure of the women from the empty tomb. There is more emphasis on the actions than the activity of Jesus, and he is presented as preeminently the crucified Messiah. The Gospel may be called a Passion narrative with an extended introduction and brief epilogue.

There is no sound reason to doubt the ancient tradition that John Mark is the author and that he gathered much of his material from the apostle Peter. The ending 16:9-20 is canonical but not originally part of the text of this Gospel. See **Gospels,** sec. 1 and **Mark,** sec. 2.

Matthew, Gospel of. A significant and enlarged revision of the Gospel of Mark, using 90 percent of the latter. Additions include the infancy narratives, the teaching of Jesus in five sections, and accounts of the resurrected Jesus. Jesus is presented as preeminently the teaching Christ (see chapters 5-7, 10, 13, 18, 24-25 and 28:19); further he is the Jewish Messiah (Christ), descended from king David, and whose life, in its details, fulfills specific OT prophecies.

Though tradition makes Matthew, the apostle, the author, it is very difficult for us to accept this in the light of the heavy dependence upon Mark. Possibly the writer gained

some of his extra material from Matthew and so gave his name to it.
See **Gospels,** sec. 1 and **Matthew,** sec. 2.

Micah, Book of. Prophecies from the reign of Jotham, Ahaz, and Hezekiah (742-687 B.C.) addressed to the two cities, Jerusalem and Samaria. Micah was a contemporary of Amos, Hosea, and Isaiah, and like them he expected God to use a pagan nation to punish his faithless covenant people. The contents are both condemnation and hope: Israel's punishment and later restoration. The famous oracle about Bethlehem, birthplace of the Messiah, is in chapter 5.
See **Micah,** sec. 2.

Nahum, Book of. Prophecies delivered after 663 (the fall of Thebes to Assyria) and before 612 B.C. (the fall of Nineveh to the Babylonians and Medes). They contain a message of doom for Nineveh, capital of Assyria. The God of Israel, despised by the Assyrians, is the Lord and Judge of the nations, and he will punish this empire and its hated capital city. This book stands in contrast to that of Jonah which (for a different historical period) portrays hope and salvation for Nineveh: Nahum (meaning comfort or compassion) lived in southwestern Judah but nothing is known of him.
See **Nineveh,** sec. 3.

Nehemiah, Book of. Together with the book of Ezra this provides us with the story of the return of the exiles from Babylon under Ezra in 458 and under Nehemiah in 445 B.C. The contents fall into 3 parts: Nehemiah's return and work as governor (1:1-7:73a); Ezra's work as reformer (7:73b-9:37, a continuation of Ezr 7-10); and Nehemiah's reforms and community (9:38-13:31).
See **Ezra, Book of,** sec. 1 and **Nehemiah,** sec. 2.

New Testament. A collection of twenty-seven books forming the second half of the Christian Bible. Written originally in Greek, it is received by the church as canon because it declares and sets forth the new covenant (testament), brought into being by the atoning death of Jesus, the Messiah. So the NT stands in contrast to and fulfillment of the OT, the book of the old covenant.

The original manuscripts of the NT are no longer extant; the most ancient text containing all twenty-seven books is called *Sinaiticus,* dating from the fourth century. However, around 5,000 ancient manuscripts containing all or part of the NT exist. By studying these scholars seek to establish the original text.

The division of the NT into chapters was made by Stephen Langton (d. 1228) and into verses by Robert Stephanus in 1551.

See **Old Testament,** sec. 1.

Numbers, Book of. The fourth book of Moses in the Pentateuch. In Hebrew it is called "In the Wilderness" but the English title derives from the censuses of the Israelites mentioned in chapters 1-4 and 26. The contents relate to thirty-eight years in the wilderness, wandering in the Sinai peninsula. The book begins with the ending of the encampment at Mount Sinai, two years after the Exodus, and ends with the arrival at the border of Canaan, forty years after the Exodus. It is a story of complaining and discontent by the people and of punishment from God.

See **Pentateuch,** sec. 1.

Obadiah, Book of. In its one chapter the destruction of Edom is foretold. The reason for this divine judgment upon the descendants of Esau is their treatment of the Israelites. They are told not to gloat over the distress of the people of Judah (being invaded by the Babylonians). This brief prophecy arises from the great theme of several prophets—the coming of "the day of the Lord," the day of judgment and deliverance. It is to be dated after 587 B.C.; nothing is known of Obadiah.

See **Edom,** sec. 3.

Old Testament. The first part of the Christian Bible, being a collection of forty-six books, received by the church as canon. The title comes from 2 Cor 3:14, "when the old covenant is read." Thirty-nine of the books were written in Hebrew and form the Hebrew Bible (Jewish canon) as fixed by the rabbis at Jamnia in about A.D. 100. The other seven exist only in Greek and are received by the Catholic church as canonical. The whole collection sets forth and explains the old covenant and leads the reader to expect the new covenant. The division into chapters and verses began in the sixteenth century.

Without the OT the NT would be a collection of books without background, context, and clarity of meaning. Thus the OT, telling of the long preparation for the Messiah, is read as sacred Scripture within the church.
See **New Testament,** sec. 1.

Papyrus. The writing material prepared from a large aquatic plant of the sedge family. The discovery of Greek papyri in Egypt over the last century has helped us to see that the Greek of the NT belonged to the general (*koine*) Greek of the period. Further, although they do not survive, the original documents of the NT were all written on papyrus rolls or sheets.

Pentateuch (Gk., "the book in five"). The five books of Genesis, Exodus, Leviticus, Numbers, and Deuteronomy, called Torah or "Book of the Law" in Judaism and "Law" in the NT. The five contain not only the detailed contents of the covenant God made through Moses with Israel but also the context of that covenant—the choice of Abraham and his descendants as God's elect people. Moses is held in Jewish tradition to be the primary author; thus "the five books of Moses." Modern scholarship, while accepting the Mosaic origin of much of the material, has looked for various strands of material (possibly documents) underlying the Pentateuch and being used by the final editors.

Four great themes are prominent in the five books: (1)

Election (God's choice of a people for himself); (2) Covenant: God's relationship with Noah (Gn 9:9); with Abraham (Gn 15:18); and with Israel (Ex 24:7); (3) Law (in the covenant with Israel); and (4) Exodus (deliverance from Egypt and into the promised land).

Peter, First and Second Epistles of. The apostle Peter wrote 1 Peter from Rome before A.D. 64 (when the persecution under Nero began) to small, scattered churches in the five Roman provinces north of the Taurus mountains (in modern Turkey). The letter deals with the gift of God's salvation in Christ and its implication, the need for good behavior by all Christians and for readiness to suffer for Christ's sake. The key theme is hope.

Second Peter was possibly written much later than 1 Peter, either by Peter or (more probably) by a disciple. The key theme is true knowledge in order to combat false teaching, especially in relation to the second coming of Christ. It has the character of a farewell message, but we do not know to whom it was originally addressed.
See **Peter,** sec. 2.

Philemon, Epistle of Paul to. A private letter to Philemon, a member of the church in Colossae. It concerns one of his slaves, Onesimus, who had run away to Rome only there to encounter Paul and become a Christian. Paul, who had come to love Onesimus, asked Philemon to receive him not merely as his returned slave but as a brother in Christ—a revolutionary idea at that time. The letter was probably sent with the Letter to the Colossians in A.D. 60-61.
See **Philemon,** sec. 2 and **Slavery,** sec. 5.

Philippians, Epistle of Paul to the. Having founded the church in Philippi in A.D. 50 (Acts 16:12ff), Paul wrote from prison (probably Ephesus A.D. 54, but possibly Rome A.D. 61-63), rejoicing in his suffering and commending his colleagues, Timothy and Epaphroditus. He also wanted to

thank the Philippians for a gift they had sent him, to seek to heal the divisions that had arisen in the membership, and to help them face trial by standing fast in the faith of Christ. The poem in celebration of the Incarnation in 2:5-11 is a high point in the letter.
See **Philippi,** sec. 3.

Prophets, Former and Latter. In the Hebrew Bible the order of the books after the Pentateuch (Torah) is the *Former* Prophets (Jos, Jgs, 1 and 2 Sm, 1 and 2 Kgs,) followed by the *Latter* Prophets (Is, Jer, Ez, and the book of the twelve minor prophets from Hos to Mal). The use of "former" was not continued in the Septuagint and Vulgate.

Proverbs, Book of. An anthology of poetry on practical piety: a textbook of wisdom for the young and all who wish to learn. Wisdom is based on "the fear of the Lord"—reverence for and obedience to God. Proverbs are generalizations, stating what is generally (not absolutely or invariably) true.

King Solomon's name appears in the full title and he was directly or indirectly responsible for two collections (10:1-22:16; 25:1-29:27) The book was, however, compiled after his reign and contains material from other wise men.
See **Wisdom Literature,** sec. 1.

Psalms, Book of. The hymnbook of the OT and made up of five books: 1-41; 42-72; 73-89; 90-106; 107-150. Each of these ends with a short doxology and the five end with the full doxology of Psalm 150. The heading of each psalm presents ancient Jewish tradition concerning that psalm but is not part of the original text.

This hymnbook of the Second Temple contains hymns from all periods, being compiled from earlier collections, including one ascribed to King David (containing seventy-three psalms), one used by the sons of Korah (eleven psalms), and one arranged by Asaph (twelve psalms). The whole collection is varied in style and subject matter, providing for use in public and private, in temple and at home, in joy and sorrow, in thanksgiving and in supplication.

The church took over the Psalms as its own primary hymnbook and thus the contents have had a profound effect on the development of Christian hymnody.

Pseudepigrapha (Gk., "books with a false title"). Those books which were excluded both from the Hebrew Bible and the longer Greek Septuagint and are thus not regarded as canonical.
See **Apocrypha** (OT), sec. 1.

Q (Quelle). The German word for "source," used by scholars to denote the material common to Matthew and Luke but not found in Mark's or John's Gospels. It represents the whole or part of a document used by the authors of Matthew and Luke; its existence remains a hypothesis.

Revelation, Book of. A message of hope for the churches of Asia in a time of persecution (c. A.D. 95). The book is a splendid example of symbolic (apocalyptic) language, presenting the trials of the Christians against Satan and evil within the larger context of Christ's victory at Calvary and the future intervention of God to inaugurate his perfect kingdom.

The author calls himself John and tells of his exile on the isle of Patmos because of his witness for Christ. He was both well known and possessed authority in the churches of the Roman province of Asia. If he was not the apostle John then he was an associate of the apostle with the same name.
See **Apocalyptic Literature,** sec. 1.

Romans, Epistle of Paul to the. Written about A.D. 57 from Corinth to a church that Paul had not founded. He viewed the church in the city of Rome (capital of a mighty empire) as

a strategic center for the expansion of the Christian mission west into Spain. Thus he provided a comprehensive statement—a kind of theological handbook—of the gospel of God's grace as he proclaimed and taught it. Important in his treatment are the themes of justification by faith (being declared righteous by God for Christ's sake alone), of the committed life of righteousness and holiness led by the Holy Spirit, and of the unity of Jewish and Gentile believers in Christ.
See **Roman Empire,** sec. 3.

Ruth, Book of. A beautiful short story set in the period of the Judges, illustrating the truth that God is the protector of the widowed and rewards faithfulness to him. Ruth, a Moabitess, is the heroine: she went to Israel and married Boaz; their first child was the grandfather of King David. We do not know who was the author or when it was written.
See **Ruth,** sec. 2.

Samuel, First and Second Books of. The religious history of Israel from c. 1075 to 975 B.C., from the end of the period of the Judges through the reign of Saul to the final years of king David. Samuel is not the author but the major figure of the first part of the narrative. The contents are: (1) Samuel (1 Sm 1:1-7:14); (2) Samuel and Saul (7:15-15:35); (3) Saul and David (16:1-31:13); (4) David, the early years (2 Sm 1:1-8:18); (5) David and his court (9:1-20:26); and (6) an appendix (21:1-24:25). Originally these two were one book and are part of what the Jews call "the former prophets." The identity of the author is not known.
See **Samuel,** sec. 2.

Septuagint (LXX). According to the legend contained in the *Letter to Aristeas,* this first Greek translation of the Hebrew Bible was completed by seventy-two scholars in seventy-two days. According to more reliable tradition, it was done by numerous scholars over a period from 250 to

150 B.C. It was intended for Jews who spoke Greek, especially for those in Alexandria, and it was the Bible used in the church in its earliest days. To the contents of the Hebrew Bible were added other books of a deuterocanonical and apocryphal kind, but not all these were accepted as canonical by the church.
See **Canon,** sec. 1.

Sirach, Book of. Not in the Hebrew Bible, it is held in high esteem by Jews and called *Ecclesiasticus* ("church book") by Christians because it was much read in the church, both for its moral teaching and within the liturgy. It contains practical wisdom—advice for a successful life in reverence for and obedience of God. It concludes with a eulogy, the praise of famous men (the worthies of Israel).

Song of Songs, The. The title means "the best of songs." A series of lyric poems on love between a man and woman, set in springtime. It is a celebration of the sacredness of marriage. Thus the book functions as a parable of the deep love of God for his people, Israel, to whom he bound himself by a holy covenant. Jews read it at the feast of Passover. For Christians it symbolizes the unity of love between Christ and his bride, the church.

Synoptic Gospels. Matthew, Mark, and Luke have been called by this name since 1774 because they lend themselves to study by their texts being placed in parallel columns to show coincidence. Many scholars believe that Matthew and Luke use not only Mark but also another source, Q.
See **Q,** sec. 1.

Talmud. The collection of Jewish civil and canonical law (a kind of extension of the Torah) consisting of the Mishnah (originally the oral law) and the Gemara (comments of Rabbis upon the Mishnah). There is the Palestinian Talmud (completed in the fourth century A.D.) and the longer Babylonian Talmud (completed in the fifth century A.D.).

They are helpful to Christian scholars because they show how Jews interpreted the Bible.

Targums. Aramaic translations of parts of the Hebrew Bible, made for Aramaic-speaking Jews before and during the time of Jesus. Because they indicate Jewish methods of interpretation they are helpful to Christian scholars.

Thessalonians, First and Second Epistles of Paul to the. Paul left behind a small and vigorous church when he left Thessalonica in A.D. 50 (Acts 17:1ff). He sent Timothy to encourage the new believers, who, on his return, told Paul the good news of their faithfulness and enthusiasm; he also explained their problems (questions about morality and about the time of the second coming of Jesus). To answer these Paul wrote 1 Thessalonians in A.D. 51.

Later in A.D. 52 he heard that they were still confused about the time of the Lord's return and so he wrote 2 Thessalonians.

See **Thessalonica,** sec. 3.

Timothy, First and Second Epistles of Paul to. These letters, with that to Titus, reveal that Paul was released from imprisonment in Rome, that he engaged in further activity in the eastern Mediterranean, and that he was arrested again and taken to Rome (where he was executed).

First Timothy was written from Macedonia in A.D. 64 when Paul was a free man. Second Timothy was written when he was a prisoner (A.D. 65-67) in Rome. Paul gave advice to his young colleague on such topics as worship, right order and discipline, and human relations within the congregations. The advice in 2 Timothy has a more urgent ring to it, because Paul is aware that his days are now numbered, but he still longs to see Timothy again.

These letters, with that to Titus, are often called the "Pastoral Epistles."

See **Timothy,** sec. 2.

Titus, Epistle of Paul to. Written by Paul in A.D. 65 after release from his first imprisonment to his colleague and friend, Titus, who looked after the churches in Crete. It provides advice concerning his role as a pastor and leader and teaching concerning Christian life and conduct.
See **Titus,** sec. 2.

Tobit, Book of. Named after its principal hero, this is a fine story, illustrating Jewish piety and morality. It has a marvelous hymn of praise in chapter 16. Set in the eighth century in Nineveh, it was probably written c. 190-170 B.C. in Aramaic and later translated into Greek. It is not in the Hebrew Bible but is in the Septuagint and is accepted as Scripture by the Catholic church. Protestants place it in the Apocrypha.

Torah (Heb., "instruction, law"). The Hebrew name for the first five books of the OT, the Pentateuch. The word has been used in Judaism to refer not only to the Pentateuch as the written law but also to the tradition of oral teaching which grew up as an explanation of the written word. This oral teaching eventually was written down to create the Mishnah.
See **Talmud,** sec. 1.

Versions of the Bible. The most important version of the Bible for Catholics is the Vulgate. This was chiefly the work of St. Jerome, being commissioned by Pope Damasus I in 382. It was the Scripture text used by church councils in the West including Vatican II.

The important English translations for Catholics are the Douay (1609), Knox (1949), RSV Catholic Edition (1965), Jerusalem Bible (1966; second ed., 1985) and the New American Bible (1970; second ed. NT, 1987).

Wisdom, Book of (Wisdom of Solomon). Written c. 100 B.C. in Alexandria, Egypt by an anonymous author. Though the language is Greek, the style is reminiscent of Hebrew verse. To emphasize his teaching, the author sometimes speaks as though he himself were the great king Solomon. The purpose of the book is to encourage faithful Jews in a time of suffering and oppression, in part caused by fellow Jews who had abandoned their faith. The central part of the book is a celebration by Solomon of divine wisdom; before this there is teaching of divine justice, and after it reflection upon God's action in history and in mercy. Over the centuries the church has made great use of the book in the Liturgy. Protestants place it in the Apocrypha.

Wisdom Literature. The books of the Hebrew (Prv, Job, Eccl) and Greek (Wis, Sir) canon, in which two broad types of practical wisdom are found: (1) short, pithy sayings providing guidelines and rules for personal happiness; (2) monologues or dialogues which face up to the problems and purpose of life. This form of literature was found throughout the ancient Near East, especially in Egypt. The distinctiveness of the biblical material is that the practical advice is given in the context of the reverence for and obedience to the Lord, the God of Israel. When prophecy came to an end, wisdom literature gained in importance—as the Book of Sirach (175 B.C.) and the Wisdom of Solomon (100 B.C.) illustrate.

Zechariah, Book of. This has 2 parts. (1) Prophecies delivered between 520 and 518 B.C. during the rebuilding of the Temple by the recently returned exiles (1-8); and (2) prophecies belonging to a later, unspecified time (9-14). Many scholars doubt that Zechariah was responsible for the second half; however, here are oracles about Israel and the nations and the future Messiah (one of the latter describes his entry into Jerusalem upon the foal of an ass, 9:9).
See **Zechariah,** sec. 2.

Zephaniah, Book of. These oracles, primarily concerning "the day of the Lord," with judgment upon the nations as well as upon Jerusalem itself, were delivered in the reign of king Josiah (640-609 B.C.). In his message of doom, the prophet also saw a future for the covenant people of God after their experience of the purifying fires of suffering (3:14-15). Possibly some of the abuses denounced by Zephaniah were removed by Josiah in the reforms of 621 B.C. See **Zephaniah,** sec. 2.

TWO

Personal Names

Aaron. Consecrated the first high priest of the people of Israel by his younger brother Moses. His descendants were priests and called the "sons of Aaron" and "house of Aaron"; they ministered at the central sanctuary.
Ex 28; Jos 21:4; Ps 115:12.

Abel (breath). The shepherd son of Adam and Eve, who was murdered by his jealous brother Cain.
Gn 4; Heb 11:4; Mt 23:35.

Abiathar (excellent father). He alone escaped Saul's massacre of the priests at Nob and joined David. With Zadok he courageously served David during Absalom's rebellion. Deposed as high priest by Solomon for supporting Adonijah's attempt to succeed David as king.
1 Sm 22:11-23; 2 Sm 15:24-37; 17:15; 1 Kgs 1-2.

Abner (father of light). Saul's cousin and commander-in-chief. He capably supported Ishbosheth's claim to the throne after Saul's death but lost favor and went over to David. He was murdered by a jealous Joab at Hebron.
1 Sm 14:50; 2 Sm 2:8; 3:6-38.

Abraham (father of multitudes). Originally known as Abram, he became the ancestor of several peoples, especially the Hebrews. Born at Ur of the Chaldees, he married Sarai (Sarah), and later moved to Haran, where his father Terah

died. Responding to God's call he journeyed to Canaan, a land that God promised to give to him and his descendants. Although both he and his wife were aged and childless, a son, Isaac, was miraculously born to them. Abraham's faith was severely tested when God ordered him to sacrifice his son at Moriah, but his willingness to obey resulted in Isaac's deliverance and the sacrifice of a ram as a substitute. Paul uses Abraham's faith to illustrate salvation by grace.
Gn 17:5; 11:27-32; 12; 15; 22; Rom 4.

Absalom (father of peace). The handsome son of David and Maacah. He killed his half-brother Amnon for raping his sister Tamar, and he was banished by David. On his return he led a rebellion against his father, but he came to an ignominious end.
2 Sm 3:3; 13-15; 18.

Achan. By stealing booty from Jericho, he brought about Israel's defeat at Ai. Stoned and cremated in a valley consequently named Achor (trouble).
Jos 7.

Adam (man, human being). The first man, formed by God of dust from the ground as the climax of creation. His disobedience led to expulsion from the garden of Eden. Died at age 930. Paul draws contrasts between Christ and Adam. Adam's union with Eve illustrates the permanence of marriage.
Gn 1:26; 2:7; 3; 5:5; Mt 19:4-6; Lk 3:38; 1 Cor 15:22, 45.

Agabus. A Christian prophet of Jerusalem, whose prediction of widespread famine was fulfilled in the reign of Claudius. At Caesarea he foretold Paul's imprisonment.
Acts 11:28; 21:10.

Agrippa. See **Herod,** sec. 2.

Ahab (father's brother). Seventh king of Israel (874-852 B.C.). Married the pagan Jezebel, princess of Sidon, for

whom he built a temple dedicated to Baal, a deity of Tyre. As a result Ahab was denounced by the prophet Elijah. Ahab defeated the Syrians but was condemned for sparing their king, Ben-hadad. Incited by Jezebel, Ahab seized Naboth's vineyard and earned Elijah's sentence of judgment to come. Misled by false prophets, Ahab met his death fighting against the Syrians.
1 Kgs 16:32; 17-22.

Ahasuerus. The Persian king, Xerxes I (485-465 B.C.). He divorced Vashti and married Esther; he rewarded Mordecai for his loyalty and hanged Haman for plotting against the Jews.
Est; Ezr 4:6.

Ahijah (Yahweh is my brother). A prophet from Shiloh who tore a new robe into twelve pieces, ten of which he gave to Jeroboam, thereby symbolizing the division of Solomon's kingdom. When Jeroboam led Israel into idolatry, Ahijah foretold the extinction of his family and the exile of Israel.
1 Kgs 11:29-40; 14:6-16.

Amos (burdened). Shepherd and sycamore-fig farmer, and a native of Tekoa, ten miles from Jerusalem, called by God to prophesy in the days of Uzziah, king of Judah, and Jeroboam II of Israel about 760 B.C.
Amos 1:1; 7:4. See also **Amos, Book of,** sec. 1.

Ananias. Three men bear this name. (1) A Jerusalem Christian who collapsed and died when his deceit over a contribution to the common fund was exposed by Peter (Acts 5:1-6); (2) a Damascus Christian who ministered to Saul of Tarsus and passed on Christ's commission to him (Acts 9:10); (3) the high priest whose malpractice when examining Paul at a meeting of the Sanhedrin earned the apostle's rebuke of "whitewashed wall" (Acts 23:2; 24:1).

Andrew (manly). Apostle. From Bethsaida in Galilee he

went to live at Capernaum in a fishing partnership with his brother Simon Peter. He was a disciple of John the Baptist before following Jesus. Andrew introduced to Jesus not only Peter, but also the boy with the loaves and fishes and some Greeks. He asked Jesus about the coming judgment and was present at the Ascension.
Mt 4:18; 10:2; Mk 1:29; Jn 1:35-44; 6:8; 12:22; Acts 1:13.

Anna (Greek form of *Hannah,* "grace"). An aged widow, of the tribe of Asher, who devoted herself to worship in the Temple. She welcomed the infant Jesus as the long-awaited Messiah. One of the seven prophetesses who prophesied to Israel. In Jewish tradition the others were Sarah, Miriam, Deborah, Huldah, Abigail, and Esther.
Lk 2:36.

Antiochus (withstander). The name of thirteen kings of the Seleucid dynasty, who ruled Asia Minor and Syria after the division of the empire of Alexander the Great. It appears frequently in First and Second Maccabees, where Antiochus IV Epiphanes (175-164 B.C.), Antiochus V Eupator (164-162 B.C.), Antiochus VI Dionysus (145-142 B.C.), and Antiochus VII Sidetes (139-129 B.C.) are specifically mentioned.
1 Mc 1:20ff; 6:17 and 7:1-4; 11:39, 57ff; 15:1ff.

Apollos. An eloquent Alexandrian Jew, deeply versed in the OT and with some knowledge of John's baptism and of Jesus, but needing further instruction by Priscilla and Aquila. From Ephesus he went to Corinth, powerfully preaching Jesus to the Jews. One clique at Corinth even took Apollos' name.
Acts 18:24-28; 1 Cor 1:12; 3:4-6; 16:12; Ti 3:13.

Aquila and Prisca (Priscilla). A Jewish-Christian leather-worker from Patmos and his wife. They were expelled from Rome by the edict of Claudius against Jews in A.D. 49.
Acts 18:1-3, 18-28; 1 Cor 16:19; Rom 16:3.

Augustus Caesar. The first Roman emperor, ruling from 31 B.C. to A.D. 14. His decree sent Joseph and Mary to Bethlehem, where Jesus was born.
Lk 2:1. See also **Roman Empire,** sec. 3.

Balaam. A prophet bribed by Balak, king of Moab, to curse the Israelites; he instead pronounced blessings.
Nm 22-24.

Barabbas (son of father). A notorious Jewish revolutionary arrested by the Romans for murder. The priests prevailed upon Pilate to release him at the Passover instead of Jesus.
Mt 27:16-17; Mk 15:7; Lk 23:18; Jn 18:40.

Barak (lightning). A Naphtalite summoned by the prophetess Deborah to rally the Israelites against the Canaanite general Sisera.
Jgs 4-5; Heb 11:32.

Barnabas (encourager). Cognomen of one of the first Christian missionaries, a member of a Jewish-Cypriot priestly family and a cousin of John Mark. He befriended Saul of Tarsus, represented the Jerusalem church at Antioch (where Gentiles were being converted), and recognized that the mission to the Gentiles was Saul's work. With Saul (Paul) he carried famine relief to Jerusalem, where the mission to Gentiles was recognized. He temporarily gave way to judaizing pressure in Antioch before joining Paul in the mission to the Gentiles.
Acts 4:36; 9:27; 11:25-26; 13-14; 15; Col 4:10; Gal 2:1, 9, 13.

Bartholomew (son of Ptolemy). One of the twelve apostles, paired with Philip.
Mt 10:3; Mk 3:18; Lk 6:14; Acts 1:13.

Baruch (blessed). Faithful servant of the prophet Jeremiah. He wrote down his master's prophecies and went into exile in Egypt with him. Jeremiah uttered a special oracle

concerning him. The canonical Book of Baruch is not by him, but his name was used for several apocryphal books, notably *The Apocalypse of Baruch.*
Jer 36:4, 10, 32; 32:11ff; 45:1ff. See **Baruch, Book of,** sec 1.

Bathsheba. Daughter of Eliam and wife of Uriah the Hittite. David plotted Uriah's death at the siege of Rabbah in order to marry her; he earned the rebuke of Nathan the prophet. In David's old age she cooperated with Nathan to secure the succession of Solomon and thus her own position as queen mother.
2 Sm 11-12; 1 Kgs 1.

Benjamin (son of the right hand). Jacob's youngest son, whose mother Rachel died at his birth. After Joseph was lost he became his father's favorite son; this fact eventually brought about the reconciliation of Joseph and the other brothers.

The tribe descended from him and bearing his name was famous for its fighting skill and left-handed slingers. The apostle Paul was a Benjaminite.
Gn 35:18, 24; 42:4; 44; 46:21; 1 Chr 8; Rom 11:1.

Boaz (by him he is mighty). Prosperous Bethlehem farmer who took the widow Ruth as his wife under levirate marriage and so became the great-grandfather of David.
Ruth 2-4; Mt 1:5.

Caiaphas. High priest in Jerusalem (A.D. 18-36), son-in-law of Annas, his predecessor. In office at the time of Jesus' trial and during the early persecution of Christians.
Jn 18:13; 11:49; Acts 4:6.

Cain. Eldest son of Adam and Eve. An agriculturist, he murdered his shepherd brother Abel out of jealousy and was exiled to the land of Nod,where he lived as a nomad.
Gn 4; 1 Jn 3:12; Heb 11:4.

Caleb. The name of several men in the OT, in particular of Caleb ben Jephunneh. He was an outstanding leader of

Judah in the period of the sojourn in the wilderness and entry into Canaan. He was both one of the twelve scouts sent to spy out the land and one of the twelve men appointed to apportion the land of Canaan to the tribes.
Nm 13:6; 14:6, 24, 30, 38; 34:19; Jos 14:6, 13, 14; 15:13-17.

Claudius. Roman emperor A.D. 41-54. A famine foretold by Agabus occurred in his reign. He banished the Jews from Rome in A.D. 49.
Acts 11:28; 18:2. See also **Roman Empire,** sec. 3.

Cornelius. A Roman centurion of the cohort stationed at Caesarea; a "God-fearer" who became the first Gentile convert to Christ.
Acts 10.

Cyrus. Persian king (Cyrus II, 559-530 B.C.); also conquered Babylon (539). He allowed the exiled Jews to return to Judea and to restore their Temple.
2 Chr 36:22; Is 44:28; 45:1; Ezr 1:1; 6:3; Dn 6:28; 10:1. See also **Persia,** sec. 3.

Dan. Son of Jacob and Rachel's handmaid Bilhah and ancestor of the tribe of Dan, which settled west of the Dead Sea but later migrated northwards.
Gn 30:6; 49:16-18; Jos 19:40-48.

Daniel. Four men bear this name. (1) The second son of David, by Abigail (1Chr 3:1); (2) exiled priestly descendant of Ithamar who returned from exile with Ezra (Ezr 8:2; Neh 10:6); (3) a man outstanding for his godly wisdom, classed with Noah and Job (Ez 14:14, 20; 28:3); (4) the fourth of the major prophets, a young Jew of noble descent deported to Babylon in 597 B.C., renamed Belteshazzar, and trained for Nebuchadnezzar's service. Interpreter of visions and a leading official in Babylon. (Dn; Mt 24:15).

Darius. Three men in the Bible bear this name. (1) Darius the Mede son of Ahasuerus. Unknown to history, he is recorded in Scripture as the man who displaced Belshazzar as king of the Chaldeans and made Daniel one of his district governors. (Dn 5:30-6:2; 9:1). (2) Darius I (521-486 B.C.), king of Persia and Babylon authorized the exiled Jews to return to Jerusalem and to rebuild the Temple, led by Jeshua and Zerubbabel (Ezr 4-6; Hg 1:1; Zec 1:1). (3) Darius II (423-408 B.C.), called Darius the Persian (Neh 12:22).

David. Youngest of Jesse's eight sons and second king of Israel, he subjugated Israel's enemies, prepared for the building of the Temple, and organized national worship. Skilled in music and in composing elegies and psalms. Ancestor of Jesus and prophet of the coming Messiah and his resurrection. "Son of David" was a title of the Messiah. 1 Sm 16-1 Kgs 2; 1 Chr 2-29; Mt 1:17; 12:3; Acts 1:16; 2:25,29.

Deborah (bee). Two women bear this name. (1) Rebekah's nurse who died at Bethel (Gn 35:8). (2) a judge-prophetess (about 1125 B.C.) who ordered Barak to lead the Israelites against Sisera. The victory song of Deborah is one of the most ancient passages in the OT (Jgs 4-5).

Delilah. A beautiful Hebrew girl from the valley of Sorek. She became the mistress of Samson and then betrayed him into the hands of the Philistines. She had his hair cut off while he slept and thus he lost his strength.
Jdg 16:4-22.

Dorcas (gazelle). Greek translation of the Aramaic name *Tabitha.* A Christian woman, prominent in the church at Joppa, who was restored to life by Peter's prayer.
Acts 9:36-41.

Eleazar (God has helped). Most OT occurrences of this common name are to the third son of Aaron, who succeeded his father as high priest. He was buried at Gibeah in Ephraim. From Eleazar were descended one of the two main

divisions of the full priesthood and almost all the high priests down to Maccabean times.
Nm 20:25-28; Jos 24:33.

Eli. High priest and predecessor of Samuel as judge in Israel. He was kind to Hannah and Samuel, but failed to discipline his unfaithful sons. The shock of their death in battle killed him.
1 Sam 1-4.

Elijah (Yahweh is God). Outstanding ninth-century prophet from Tishbe in Gilead who consistently opposed Ahab and Ahaziah and the worship of Baal in their reigns. His dramatic translation into heaven was observed by his successor Elisha.
1 Kgs 17-21; 2 Kgs 1-2; Mal 4:5-6; Mt 17:3, 10-12.

Elisha (God is salvation). Ninth-century prophet in Israel and successor to Elijah. A native of Abel-meholah in the Jordan valley, he ministered for fifty years through the reigns of Ahab, Ahaziah, Jehoram, Jehu, Jehoahaz, and Jehoash.
1 Kgs 19:16-21; 2 Kgs 2-9; 13; Lk 4:27.

Elizabeth. Wife of the priest Zechariah and mother of John the Baptist; a relative of Mary, the mother of Jesus.
Lk 1:5-57.

Ephraim (fruitful). Second son of Joseph and Asenath, he was chosen before his brother Manasseh by his grandfather Jacob.
Gn 41:51-52; 48.

Esau (hairy). Isaac's favorite of his twin sons. Although the elder, his inferiority to his brother Jacob was foretold at birth and unwittingly confirmed by Isaac's dying blessing. Ancestor of the Edomites, chronic antagonists of the Israelites.
Gn 25:23-34; 27:22-29; 36:9; Nm 20:18; 1 Kgs 11:14.

Esther. Queen of Ahasuerus (Xerxes, 486-465 B.C.); her Jewish name was Hadassah.
Est. See **Esther, Book of,** sec. 1.

Eve (life). The first woman, wife of Adam and mother of Cain, Abel, and Seth.
Gn 3:20; 4:1; 1 Tm 2:13; 2 Cor 11:3.

Ezekiel (God strengthens). Son of Buzi, departed to Babylon with other exiled Jews in 597 B.C. His wife had died during the seige of Jerusalem. Five years after settling at Tel-abib by the river Chebar, God called him to be a prophet.
Ez 1:2-3; 24:2, 15-18. See **Ezekiel, Book of,** sec. 1.

Ezra (help). A priestly Jewish exile sent by Artaxerxes I to Jerusalem in 458 B.C. to establish the uniform observance of Jewish law in the land. Many fellow exiles went with him, bringing valuable treasure for the reestablishment of the Temple. After dealing with the problem of mixed marriages he apparently returned to the Persian king. In 444 B.C. he was back in Jerusalem publicly reading the Law. He is the founding figure of postexilic Judaism.
Ezr 9-10; Neh 8. See **Ezra, Book of,** sec. 1.

Felix (happy). Procurator of Judea (A.D. 52-59). In A.D. 55 he put down a riot instigated by an Egyptian messianic pretender. Hoping for a bribe he kept Paul in prison for two years, even though he knew that he was innocent. Recalled by the emperor Nero he left Paul in jail in order to please the Jews.
Acts 23:24-26; 24.

Festus, Porcius. Successor to Felix as procurator of Judea and a friend of Herod Agrippa II. When Paul realized that his rightful release would again be obstructed he appealed over the head of the procurator to the emperor in Rome.
Acts 24:27; 25:9-13.

Gabriel (God's mighty one). Archangel commissioned to

deliver historic messages from God to mankind. He announced the births of John the Baptist and Jesus.
Dan 8:16; 9:21; Lk 1:19, 26.

Gamaliel (God's reward). Two men bear this name. (1) Son of Pedahzur, a leader of the tribe of Manasseh who assisted in Moses' census in the wilderness (Nm 1:10; 2:20; 7:54, 59); (2) a liberal Pharisee and a leading member of the Sanhedrin who advised this council not to take precipitate action against the apostles (Acts 5:34; 22:3).

Gideon (hewer, warrior). A judge or charismatic warrior-leader of the Israelites, especially in their expulsion of the invading Midianites. He received special signs from God—a sacrifice set alight and a fleece wet with dew. He gave the land peace for forty years.
Jgs 6-8; Heb 11:32.

Gog. A future king of Magog, Meshech, and Tubal, prophesied by Ezekiel, who will lead his armies against Israel.
Ez 38-39; Rev 20:8.

Goliath. A hero of the Philistines who stood over nine feet in height. He was killed by David in single combat.
1 Sm 17.

Habakkuk. One of the twelve minor prophets who addressed Judah at the end of the seventh century B.C. He faced the problem of how the holy and righteous God could use the heathen Chaldeans to punish his elect people, Israel.
See **Habakkuk, Book of,** sec. 1.

Hagar. Egyptian handmaid to Sarah and servant in the household of Abraham. Because Sarah was childless, Hagar was given to Abraham who had a son by her. When Hagar was pregnant with Ishmael she fled; but, after an encounter with God, she returned to Abraham's household. Later, however, she was expelled along with her son. The apostle

Paul used her story as an allegory to teach freedom from the Law of Moses.
Gn 16:1-16; 21:9-17; Gal 4:24-25.

Haggai. One of the twelve minor prophets who addressed the returned exiles in Jerusalem about 520 B.C. Possibly he himself had been in exile with them.
See **Haggai, Book of,** sec. 1.

Ham. Son of Noah, brother of Japheth and Shem, and father of Canaan. He survived the Flood to become the ancestor of various peoples.
Gn 5:32; 6:10; 9:18-27; 10:6-20.

Haman. The villain of the Book of Esther. As grand vizier appointed by king Xerxes, he plotted to massacre the Jews when Mordecai refused to bow down before him. Through the intervention of Queen Esther, he was eventually hanged at the very gallows that had been prepared by him for Mordecai.
See **Esther, Book of,** sec. 1.

Hannah. The favored of the two wives of Elkanah. In answer to her prayer and vow, she conceived and gave birth to Samuel, whom she dedicated to the Lord. Afterwards she had other children. A song or psalm is attributed to her, upon which Mary's *Magnificat* is based.
1 Sm 1 and 2

Herod. Three men bear this name. (1) Herod the Great, who was appointed procurator of Judea by Julius Caesar in 47 B.C.; later he was given the title, "King of the Jews" and reigned till 4 B.C. (Mt 2; Lk 1:5). (2) Herod the Ethnarch (Archelaus), his son. He ruled Judea from 4 B.C. to A.D. 6. (Mt 2:22). (3) Herod the king (Herod Agrippa I), grandson of Herod the Great. He ruled Galilee, Judea and Samaria from A.D. 34-44 (Acts 12). His son (Herod) Agrippa II ruled from A.D. 50 (Acts 25:13-26:32).

Hezekiah (Yahweh is strength). King of Judah, 716-687 B.C.

He was a reformer of religion and sought to remove idolatry from the land. He also sought to resist the attempts of Assyria to subjugate Judah and Jerusalem; in his resistance he experienced God's supernatural intervention.
2 Kgs 18-20; 2 Chr 29-32; Is 36-39.

Hiram (my brother is the exalted god). Phoenician king of Tyre (979-945 B.C.). He sent materials and craftsmen both to David for the building of his palace and to Solomon for the building of the Temple in Jerusalem. From his reign is to be dated the expansion of the Phoenician navy, leading to the creation of cities and markets in the Mediterranean and Africa.
1 Kgs 5:11-26; 7:13-45; 9:11-27.

Hosea (salvation). A prophet and citizen of the northern kingdom of Israel, he prophesied in the reign of Jeroboam II. He used his unhappy experience of marriage in a creative manner to illustrate God's love for unfaithful Israel.
See **Hosea, Book of,** sec. 1.

Isaac (he laughs). Son of Abraham and Sarah, born when his parents were old, according to God's promise. As a boy he was on the verge of being offered by his father as a sacrifice when God intervened to save him. Later he married Rebekah and by her had twin sons, Esau and Jacob. He was retiring and contemplative by nature.
Gn 21-22; 24-28; 35:27-29; Gal 4:28; Heb 11:9, 20.

Isaiah (Yahweh has saved). A major prophet who lived in Jerusalem during the reigns of Uzziah, Jotham, Ahaz, and Hezekiah from 742 to at least 701 B.C. His call to prophesy came when he was in the Temple and involved a vision of God's glory. He was married to a prophetess and had two sons, to whom he gave names indicating what God was going to do: Shearjashub (Is 7:3) and Mahershalalhashbaz (Is 8:3).
See **Isaiah, Book of,** sec. 1.

Ishmael (God hears). The son of Abraham by Hagar, the Egyptian slave. He was circumcised when thirteen years old; and, three years later, after mocking his baby half-brother, Isaac, he was banished with his mother. They nearly perished from thirst but were miraculously led to a well. Ishmael became an archer, married an Egyptian, and fathered twelve princes. Esau married one of his daughters.
Gn 16:11-16; 17:18-26; 21:11; 25:9-16; 28:9; 36:3.

Israel. See **Jacob,** sec. 2.

Israel, Kings of.

The Northern Kingdom of Israel

King	*Dates*	*Biblical Reference*
Jeroboam I	931-910 B.C.	1 Kgs 12:1-14:20; 2 Chr 10; 13
Nadab	910-909 B.C.	1 Kgs 15:25-32
Baasha	909-886 B.C.	1 Kgs 15:16-21; 16:1-7; 2 Chr 16:1-6
Elah	886-885 B.C.	1 Kgs 16:8-14
Zimri	885-884 B.C.	1 Kgs 16:15-20
Tibni	884-880 B.C.	1 Kgs 16:21-22
Omri	880-874 B.C.	1 Kgs 16:22-28
Ahab	874-853 B.C.	1 Kgs 16:29-22:40; 2 Chr 18:1-34
Ahaziah	853-852 B.C.	1 Kgs 22:52-2 Kgs 1:18
Joram	852-841 B.C.	2 Kgs 3:1-9:26
Jehu	841-814 B.C.	2 Kgs 9:1-10:36
Jehoahaz	814-798 B.C.	2 Kgs 13:1-9

Jehoash	798-782 B.C.	2 Kgs 13:10-13
Jeroboam II	782-753 B.C.	2 Kgs 14:23-29
Zechariah	753-752 B.C.	2 Kgs 15:8-12
Shallum	752-752 B.C.	2 Kgs 15:13-16
Menahem	752-742 B.C.	2 Kgs 15:17-22
Pekahiah	742-740 B.C.	2 Kgs 15:23-26
Pekah	740-732 B.C.	2 Kgs 15:27-31
Hoshea	732-723 B.C.	2 Kgs 17:1-41

Destroyed by Assyrians 723 B.C.

Jacob (God guards). Son of Isaac and Rebekah, and the (younger) twin brother of Esau. He gained his father's special blessing by pretending to be Esau and then fled to Haran from his brother's wrath. On the way he had a vision of a ladder connecting heaven and earth with angels descending and ascending. In Haran he married two wives, Leah and Rachel, and had eleven sons. Returning to his own land with his family and possessions, he had a strange encounter with an unknown man or angel and through this experience God gave him the new name of Israel. His sons became the ancestors of the twelve tribes.
Gn 25:21-34; 27-35; 37:1; 42-49.

Jacob, Sons of.

The Sons of Jacob

(Gn 29:32-35; 30:17-21)	By Leah:	Reuben Simeon Levi Judah Issachar Zebulun

(Gn 30:4-8)	By Bilhah:	Dan Naphtali
(Gn 30:10-12)	By Zilpah:	Gad Asher
(Gn 30:22-24; 35:18)	By Rachel:	Joseph Benjamin

Leah and Rachel were wives; Bilhah and Zilpah were concubines.

James. Three men bear this name. (1) James son of Zebedee, brother of John, disciple and apostle, a "son of thunder." He was a martyr under Herod Agrippa I (Mt 4:21-22; 17:1; Mk 5:37; 10:35-41; Acts 12:2). (2) James son of Alphaeus, disciple and apostle, known as "James the younger" (Mt 10:3; Mk 15:40; Acts 1:13). (3) James "brother of the Lord," a relative of Jesus, who became leader of the church in Jerusalem and to whom is ascribed the Letter of James. (Mt 13:55; Acts 12:17; 1 Cor 15:7).

Japheth. Son of Noah and brother of Shem and Ham. He survived the Flood to become the ancestor of various peoples.
Gn 5:32; 9:18-23; 10:1-5; 1 Chr 1:4.

Jephthah (God opens the womb). A "judge" or charismatic leader of the Israelites, especially against the Ammonites. His rule was marred by the sacrifice of his daughter as a burnt offering in order to keep a vow he made to God.
Jgs 11:1-12:7.

Jeremiah (Yahweh establishes). A major prophet in Judah from about 626 to 587 B.C. He prophesied under the last five kings of Judah. When Jerusalem fell to Nebuchadnezzar, he was not deported to Babylon; however, he was later forced by his countrymen to go down into Egypt.
2 Chr 35:25; 36:12, 21-22. See **Jeremiah, Book of,** sec. 1.

Jeroboam (may the people increase). First king of the southern kingdom of Israel (931-910 B.C.). In the reign of Solomon he led a revolt of the northern tribes against the king's harsh treatment of them. This led to his exile in Egypt. After the death of Solomon, he was elected by popular choice as king over the ten tribes and thus the division of Israel and Judah as two separate kingdoms began. However, in opposing king Rehoboam of Jerusalem and setting up the northern kingdom, he incurred the divine wrath by building shrines at Dan and Bethel and creating a non-levitical priesthood.
1 Kgs 12-14.

Jeroboam II. Fourth king (782-753 B.C.) of Jehu's dynasty and one of the northern kingdom's most illustrious rulers. His reign was one of economic prosperity but not of sound religion. Amos delivered severe prophecies against Israel during his reign.
Amos 5-7; 1 Kgs 14:23ff.

Jesus (form of *Joshua*, "Savior"). Conceived by the Holy Spirit in the womb of the virgin Mary, Jesus was born in Bethlehem, thereby fulfilling ancient prophecy. He was taken by Mary and Joseph into Egypt for several years and then raised by them in Nazareth in Galilee. His education and upbringing were those of a pious Jew. Baptized by John the Baptist, he began his ministry in Galilee and Judea. He preached, taught, healed the sick, and gathered around him a company of disciples and apostles in service of the kingdom of God. Eventually his opponents brought him to trial and handed him over to the Roman authorities for death by crucifixion. He rose from death on the third day following his burial and appeared to his disciples regularly for the next forty days. He is now in heaven in his resurrected body as the exalted king, priest, and prophet, and he will come again to judge the living and the dead.

Jezebel. Daughter of Ethbaal, king of Sidon, who became the wife of Ahab, king of Israel. She was an ardent devotee of Baal; at her suggestion Ahab introduced the worship of Baal and Asherah into Israel. She caused the prophets of Yahweh to be slain and attempted to kill Elijah. She suffered a violent death predicted by Elijah.
1 Kgs 16:31; 18:4, 13, 19; 19:1-2; 21; 2 Kgs 9:30-37.
See **Baal,** sec. 4.

Job. An outstandingly righteous man who lived in the land of Uz, east of Palestine. He lost wealth, children and health in a series of disasters, but he refused to curse God. He gained insight into the power and wisdom of God, and in the end God healed him and restored much of what he had lost.
Ez 14:14, 20; Jas 5:11. See **Job, Book of,** sec. 1.

Joel (Yahweh is God). There are thirteen men of this name, including the author of the Book of Joel, who was a son of Pethuel.
1 Sam 8:2; 1 Chr 4:35; 5:4, 8, 12; 6:34, 36, 38; 7:3; 11:38; 15:7, 11, 17; 27:20; Ezr 10:43; Neh 11:9; Joel 1:1. See **Joel, Book of,** sec. 1.

John (Yahweh has been gracious). Ten men of this name. (1) The father of Mattathias (1 Mc 2:1). (2) The eldest son of Mattathias (1 Mc 2:2; 9:36, 38, 42). (3) The son of Accos and father of Eupolemus (1 Mc 8:17; 2 Mc 4:11). (4) An envoy of the Jews sent to Lysias (2 Mc 11:17). (5) The son of Simon Maccabeus, known as John Hyrcanus (1 Mc 13:53; 16:1, 23). (6) The father of Simon Peter (Jn 1:42; 21:15-17; Mt 16:17). (7) John the Baptist, son of Zachariah and Elizabeth. Around 27 A.D. he appeared as a prophetic preacher in the wilderness near the Jordan. He baptized Jews, including Jesus. After imprisonment, he was beheaded (Mt 3:1-11; 14:1-12; Mk 1:4-6; Lk 1:5-25, 57-80; 7:18-33). (8) John the apostle, son of Zebedee and brother of James. He is either the author or the inspiration behind the Gospel,

Epistles, and Revelation that bear his name, known as the Johannine literature (Mt 4:21-22; 10:2; 17:1; Mk 3:17; 5:37; 10:35-41; 14:33; Lk 9:49; Jn 19:26-27; Acts 3-4; Gal 2:9; Rev 1). (9) John Mark, identified with Mark the evangelist (Acts 12:12, 25). (10) A Jewish leader who called the apostles Peter and John to account (Acts 4:6).

Jonah (dove). A prophet in the reign of Jeroboam II (eighth century B.C.). He is also the hero of the book which is the fifth of the Minor Prophets.
2 Kgs 14:25; Jon 1:1; See **Jonah, Book of,** sec. 1.

Jonathan (Yahweh has given). Eldest son of king Saul and bosom friend of David. A great warrior, he was killed in battle against the Philistines. David wrote a lament for him.
1 Sm 13-14; 18-20; 23:16-18; 31:2; 2 Sm 1.

Joseph (May Yahweh add). Fourteen men bear this name. (1) The eleventh of Jacob's twelve sons and the elder son of Rachel. He was sold as a slave into Egypt by his brothers but there he became an interpreter of dreams and superintendent of the royal granaries. He invited his family to come and live in Egypt (Gn 30:24; 37-50). (2) The father of the spy of the tribe of Issachar (Nm 13:7). (3) A son of Asaph and head of a group of musicians in David's reign (1 Chr 25:2, 9). (4) An ancestor of Jesus Christ who lived before the Exile (Lk 3:30). (5) A son of Binnui (Zaccai, in JB) who took a foreign wife (Ezr 10:42). (6) A priest of the family of Shebaniah (Neh 12:14). (7) Son of Mattathias and ancestor of Jesus Christ (Lk 3:24-25). (8) Son of Zechariah, who disobeyed Judas Maccabeus (1 Mc 5:18, 55-62). (9) The husband of Mary, mother of Jesus (Mt 1-2; Lk 1:27; 2:1-16). (10) A relative of Jesus (Mt 13:55). (11) Brother of James the younger (Mt 27:56; Mk 15:40). (12) A Jew of Arimathea, a member of the Sanhedrin, who buried the body of Jesus (Mt 27:57-60; Mk 15:43; Lk 23:50-53; Jn 19:38). (13) A Christian called Barsabbas and Justus who was a disciple of

Jesus from the beginning (Acts 1:23). (14) The personal name of Barnabas (Acts 4:36).

Joshua (Yahweh is salvation). Two men bear this name. (1) The successor of Moses and hero of the book of Joshua. He served under Moses in the period in the wilderness and then led the Israelites into Canaan and divided the land among the tribes (Ex 17:9-13; Nm 13-14; Jos). (2) The high priest in Jerusalem after the Exile and under the leadership of Zerubbabel. The prophets Haggai and Zechariah refer to him (Ezr 2:2, 36; 3:8-9; 5:2; Neh 7:7, 39; 12:2).

Josiah (May Yahweh give). King of Judah (640-609 B.C.) from the age of eight. He repaired the Temple and instituted religious reforms. He was killed in battle against the Egyptians.
2 Kgs 21:24-23:30; 2 Chr 33:25-35:27; Jer 22:11-16.

Judah (Let God be praised). Eight men bear this name. It is primarily the name of the fourth son of Jacob and Leah and the tribe named for him.
Gn 29:35; 37:26-27; 38; 49:9-10; Num 26:19-21; 1 Chr 2:3-6; Ez 3:9; 10:23; Neh 11:9; 12:8, 34, 36.

The Southern Kingdom of Judah

King	*Dates*	*Biblical Reference*
Rehoboam	931-913 B.C.	1 Kgs 11:43-14:31; 2 Chr 9:31-13:7
Abijam	913-911 B.C.	1 Kgs 14:31-15:8
Asa	911-870 B.C.	1 Kgs 15:8-22:47; 2 Chr 13:23-16:13
Jehoshaphat	870-848 B.C.	1 Kgs 22:2-51; 2 Chr 17:1-21:1
Jehoram (Joram)	848-841 B.C.	2 Kgs 1:17; 8:16-24; 2 Chr 21:1-20

Ahaziah	841 B.C.	2 Kgs 8:24-29; 1 Chr 22:1-9
Athaliah	841-835 B.C.	2 Kgs 11:1-20; 2 Chr 22:10-23:21
Joash	835-796 B.C.	2 Kgs 12:1-22; 2 Chr 24:1-27
Amaziah	796-767 B.C.	2 Kgs 14:1-22; 2 Chr 25:1-28
Azariah	767-740 B.C.	2 Kgs 14:21-22; 15:1-7; 2 Chr 26:1-23
Jotham	740-732 B.C.	2 Kgs 15:32-38; 2 Chr 27:1-9
Ahaz	732-716 B.C.	2 Kgs 16:1-20; 2 Chr 28:1-27
Hezekiah	716-687 B.C.	2 Kgs 18:1-20:21; 2 Chr 29:1-32:33
Manasseh	687-643 B.C.	2 Kgs 21:1-18; 2 Chr 33:1-20
Amon	643-641 B.C.	2 Kgs 21:19-26; 2 Chr 33:21-25
Josiah	640-609 B.C.	2 Kgs 22:1-23:30; 2 Chr 34:1-35:26
Jehoahaz	609 B.C.	2 Kgs 23:31-35; 2 Chr 36:2-4
Jehoiakim	609-597 B.C.	2 Kgs 23:36-24:7; 2 Chr 36:5-8
Jehoiachin	597 B.C.	2 Kgs 24:8-17; 25:27-30; 2 Chr 36:9-10
Zedekiah	597-587 B.C.	2 Kgs 24:18-25:7 2 Chr 36:11-14

Destroyed by Babylonians 587 B.C.

Judas (Gk. form of "Judah"). There are nine men who bear this name. (1) Judas Maccabeus, third of the five sons of Mattathias and successful military leader of the faithful Jews, 166-160 B.C. (1 Mc 2-9). (2) Son of Chalphi, who stood by Jonathan Maccabeus at Hazor (1 Mc 11:70). (3) Son of Simon Maccabeus and a commander of the Jewish army 137-134 B.C. (1 Mc 16). (4) Judas of Galilee, who led an insurrection against Rome in A.D. 6 (Acts 5:37). (5) Judas Iscariot, the disciple who betrayed Jesus and then committed suicide (Mt 10:4; 26:14-15; 27:3-6; Jn 12:4-6; 13:21-30; Acts 1:16-19). (6) Judas, the apostle, also called Thaddeus (Mk 3:18; Lk 6:16; Jn 14:22). (7) A relative of Jesus (Mt 13:55; Mk 6:3). (8) A Christian of Damascus with whom Paul lodged after his conversion (Acts 9:11). (9) Judas Barsabbas, a leader of the church in Jerusalem (Acts 15:22, 27, 32).

Jude (Judas). Author of the Letter of Jude and "brother of James." The same as Judas (6) or (7) above.
See **Jude, Epistle of,** sec. 1.

Judith (Jewess). The heroine of the Book of Judith. She promised her people, who were invaded by the Assyrians, that they would be liberated. After fasting and prayer she put on her best garments, went to the Assyrian camp and killed the commander-in-chief, Holofernes, as he lay drunk. Hearing of his death, the Assyrians panicked and were defeated by the Jews.
Jdt 8-16. See **Judith, Book of,** sec. 1.

Korah. Four men bear this name. (1) A son of Esau (Gn 36:5, 14, 18); (2) a son of Hebron (1 Chr 2:43); (3) a grandson of Kohath and ancestor of a group of musicians (1 Chr 6:22, 37; Ps 44-49); (4) a Levite who rebelled against Moses and Aaron and was punished by God (Nm 16).

Laban (white). Descendant of Abraham's brother, Nahor; son of Bethuel; brother of Rebekah and uncle and father-in-law of Jacob. He lived in Haran. He showed self-interest and duplicity in his dealings with Jacob, taking advantage of his love for Rachel, his daughter.
Gn 22:20-23; 24:47ff; 27:43; 28:2-5; 29-31.

Lazarus. Two men bear this name. (1) The beggar in the parable of Lk 16:19-31; (2) brother of Martha and Mary of Bethany, whom Jesus raised from the dead (Jn 11:1-12:11).

Leah. Elder daughter of Laban of Haran. Jacob was forced to marry her as he worked for Laban and waited to marry her younger sister, Rachel. She was the mother of Reuben, Simeon, Levi, Judah, Issachar, Zebulun, and Dinah, and thus regarded as a mother of the house of Israel.
Gn 29-31; 49:31; Ru 4:11.

Levi. Four men bear this name. (1) Third son of Jacob and Leah, who died in Egypt. The Levites are his descendants (Gn 29:34; 34:25-31; 49:5-7; Ex 6:16). (2), (3) Two ancestors of Jesus (Lk 3:24, 29-30). (4) Another name for Matthew, disciple and apostle (Mk 2:14-17; Lk 5:27-32).

Lot. Son of Abraham's youngest brother, Haran. He accompanied Abram and Sarai from Ur to Haran, into Canaan, to Egypt and back to Canaan. He selfishly and foolishly chose to live in Sodom, from where he had to be twice rescued. He fathered children by his two daughters and they became the ancestors of the Moabites and Ammonites.
Gn 11:27, 31; 12:4-5; 13:1-4; 14:12, 16; 19:1-38; Dt 2:9, 19.

Luke. Friend and companion of Paul, a physician, and the author of a Gospel and Acts. Speaks of "we" in the latter because he traveled with Paul.
Col 4:14; 2 Tm 4:11; Phlm 24; Acts 16:10-17; 20:5-21:18; 27:1-28:16.

Maccabee (hammer). Nickname of Judas, son of Mattathias, also extended to cover his brothers, who succeeded him in the leadership of the Jews.
See **Maccabees, Books of,** sec. 1.

Malachi (my messenger). A prophet and author of the last book of the OT. He ministered in the mid-fifth century B.C.
See **Malachi, Book of,** sec. 1.

Manasseh. Name of two men. (1) Eldest son of Joseph, born in Egypt of an Egyptian mother, Asenath. He was adopted, with his brother Ephraim, by Jacob, as his son. Thus Manasseh became one of the tribes of Israel (Gn 41:51; 46:20; 48:1-20; Nm 1:34-35; 26:29-34; 1 Ch 7:14-19). (2) Son and successor of Hezekiah as king of Judah (686-642 B.C.). At least the first part of his reign was wicked and apostate but there is some evidence that after a deportation to Babylon (where he repented) he became a better ruler.
2 Kgs 21:1-17; 2 Ch 33:10-23

Mark (John). Son of Mary of Jerusalem, cousin of Barnabas, evangelist and missionary, colleague of Barnabas and Paul, to whom is traditionally ascribed the Gospel of Mark.
Mk 14:51; Acts 12:12, 25; 13:13; 15:36-41; Col 4:10; 2 Tm 4:11; Phlm 24; 1 Pt 5:13.

Martha. Sister of Mary and Lazarus of Bethany and disciple of Jesus.
Lk 10:38-42; Jn 11:1-12:11.

Mary. (Gk form of Heb "Miriam"). Six women bear this name in the NT. (1) Mary, mother of Jesus. As a virgin she miraculously conceived before marrying Joseph. She gave birth to Jesus, whom she knew was the Messiah of Israel. From Bethlehem, where she gave birth, the family had to flee to Egypt, but later they settled in Nazareth in Galilee. Mary is mentioned several times in the Gospels, including her attendance at the crucifixion (Mt 1:18-25; 2:11; 13:55; Lk 1-2; Jn 2:1-11; 19:25-27; Acts 1:14). (2) Mary Magdalene.

Jesus cast seven devils out of her; she became his devoted and supportive disciple. She was present at the crucifixion, visited his tomb and witnessed the resurrection (Mk 16:9; Lk 8:2; 24:10; Jn 20:1-18). (3) Mary of Bethany. Sister of Martha and brother of Lazarus, who was eager to learn from Jesus (Lk 10:38-42; Jn 11:1-12:11). (4) Mary, the wife of Clopas (Jn 19:25). (5) Mary, mother of John Mark. In her home the church of Jerusalem met in its early days (Acts 12:12). (6) Mary of Rome, a member of the church in the capital city (Rom 16:6).

Matthew (gift of Yahweh). Also called Levi, he was a tax collector for the Roman authorities before becoming a disciple and apostle of Jesus. He gave his name to the first Gospel in the NT.
Mt 9:9-13; 10:3; Lk 5:27-32.

Matthias. Chosen to be an apostle to fill the place vacated by Judas Iscariot.
Acts 1:21-26.

Melchizedek (king of righteousness). A king and priest of God Most High, who met and blessed Abraham after a battle. The Letter to the Hebrews states that Jesus is a king and priest "of the order of Melchizedek."
Gn 14:18-20; Ps 110:4; Heb 5:6-10.

Micah (who is like Yahweh?). The name of seven men, the best-known being the prophet who ministered in the eighth century B.C. in the reigns of Jotham, Ahaz, and Hezekiah. He was a contemporary of Hosea and Isaiah.
1 Chr 5:5; 8:34-35; 9:15; 23:20; 24:24-25; 2 Chr 34:20; Jgs 17-18; Mic 1:1; Jer 26:18. See **Micah, Book of,** sec. 1.

Micaiah (who is like Yahweh?). A prophet of northern Israel, son of Imlah. Nothing is known of him except his single interview with king Ahab. Possibly the unknown prophet of 1 Kgs 20:35ff.
1 Kgs 22:8ff; 2 Chr 18:7-27.

Michael (who is like God?). The name of ten men and also of an archangel, who was the guardian of Israel.
Nm 13:13; 1 Chr 5:11-16; 6:40; 7:3; 8:16; 12:20; 27:18; 2 Chr 21:2; Ezr 8:8; Dan 10:21; 12:1; Jude 9; Rev 12:7.

Miriam. Sister of Aaron and Moses. She was a prophetess and after the deliverance of the Exodus she led the women in singing and dancing.
Ex 2:4-8; 15:20-21; Nm 12; 20:1.

Moab. Son of Lot by an incestuous union with his eldest daughter; ancestor of the Moabites.
Gn 19:37; Ex 15:15.

Mordecai. A Jewish exile, living in the Persian capital, Susa, where he was employed in the palace and uncle of Esther, the queen. He refused to bow down before Haman, the vizier, who then plotted to kill all Jews. After succeeding Haman as vizier, he was able to protect his fellow Jews. The Jewish feast of Purim was linked with the "day of Mordecai."
2 Mc 15:36. See **Esther, Book of,** sec. 1.

Moses. Prophet of Yahweh and leader and legislator of the Hebrews in the Exodus from Egypt to Sinai. A Levite, he became the adopted son of an Egyptian princess and was brought up as an Egyptian while his own people lived as slaves. He fled to Midian, where he received God's clear call to be the leader of the Hebrews. Returning to Egypt, he negotiated with Pharaoh and eventually led his people away from slavery, through the Red Sea, and into the Sinai Peninsula. God made a covenant with the Hebrews (Israelites) through Moses and gave to them his Law. He handed on the leadership to Joshua and when he had blessed Israel he climbed Mount Nebo to see the promised land before he died.
Ex 2-40; Lv; Nm; Dt; Lk 9:28-36. See **Pentateuch,** sec. 1.

Naaman (pleasant). A military commander of the Syrian army in the reign of Ben-hadad. Afflicted by leprosy he went

to see Elisha, prophet of the God of Israel. Elisha caused him to bathe in the dirty river Jordan and he was healed. Thus he worshipped the God of Israel.
2 Kgs 5:1-27; Lk 4:27.

Nahum (God is compassionate). The name of two men. (1) A prophet born at Elkosh who prophesied in the late seventh century B.C. to Judah (See **Nahum, Book of,** sec. 1). (2) An ancestor of Christ. Lk 3:25.

Naomi (my delight). Widow of Elimelech, with whom she had moved to Moab from Israel with her sons. They married Moabite girls, who like Naomi, were soon widows. One of them, Ruth, returned with Naomi (calling herself Mara, "bitter") to the land of Israel. Here Naomi arranged the marriage of Ruth with her kinsman, Boaz.
Ru 1-4.

Nathan (God has given). The name of six men, the best known being the prophet of the Lord who addressed both David and Solomon.
2 Sm 5:14; 7:1-17; 1 Kgs 1; 1 Chr 2:36; 11:38; 17; Ezr 8:16; 10:39.

Nathanael (God has given). A disciple, and if he is also called Bartholomew, then an apostle as well.
Jn 1:45-51; 21:2. See **Bartholomew,** sec. 2.

Nebuchadnezzar. King of Babylon, 605-562 B.C. He intervened in the affairs of Judah and was responsible for the destruction of Jerusalem and the taking of many Jews into captivity in Babylon.
2 Kgs 24-25; 2 Chr 36; Jer 21:2; 52:4-30; Ez 26:7-14; 29:17-21; Dn 1-4.

Nehemiah (Yahweh has comforted). The name of three men who returned from Exile to Jerusalem. The most important was the son of Hacaliah, from whom the Book of Nehemiah takes its name. He was a cupbearer to King Artaxerxes I of Persia; and, with the king's approval, he traveled to Jeru-

salem in order to rebuild its walls and encourage the practice of true religion.
Ezr 2:2; Neh 3:16; 7:7. See **Nehemiah, Book of,** sec. 1.

Nicodemus (victor over the people). A Pharisee and member of the supreme Jewish Council. He had an important conversation with Jesus and, together with Joseph of Arimathea, had Jesus buried.
Jn 3:1-21; 7:50-52; 19:39-42.

Noah. The last of the ten patriarchs who lived before the Flood. God made a covenant with him, and in the ark he and his family survived the deluge to begin the repopulation of the earth.
Gn 6-9; 1 Pt 3:20; Lk 17:26-27.

Obadiah. The name of twelve men; they include the prophet responsible for the fourth book of the Minor Prophets and the governor of Ahab's palace who protected the Lord's prophets from Jezebel's vengeance.
1 Kgs 18:3-4; 1 Chr 3:21; 7:3; 8:38; 9:44; 12:9; 2 Chr 17:7; 34:12; Neh 10:5; Ob 1.
See **Obadiah, Book of,** sec. 1.

Othniel. First of the charismatic judges of the tribes of Israel after their settlement in Canaan.
Jos 15:16-17; Jdg 3:7-11.

Paul (little) formerly **Saul** (asked of God). Apostle and missionary of Jesus Christ to the non-Jews of the Mediterranean world. His letters to churches and friends occupy a large part of the NT. As a learned Pharisee, he enthusiastically opposed Christianity until he had a vision of the exalted Jesus as he journeyed towards Damascus. He became a Christian and after quiet preparation he began his life's work as apostle, evangelist, teacher, and ambassador of Christ. He insisted that non-Jews could become genuine Christians without having to become also converts to

Judaism. He was executed in Rome by Nero about A.D. 67. Acts 7:58; 9-28. See **Epistle,** sec. 1.

Peter (rock) also **Cephas** (Aram., "rock"), **Simon** (Simeon). A Galilean fisherman and disciple of Jesus. He became the leader of the apostles and the early church. According to tradition he was crucified upside-down in Rome. Although he disowned Jesus at his trial, he later repented and was reinstated by the resurrected Jesus. On the day of Pentecost, Peter preached to the crowds concerning Jesus, crucified and risen. From that time onwards his life was spent in the service of Christ and his gospel, preaching and teaching from Jerusalem to Rome. Two letters in the NT bear his name.
Mt 4:18-19; 10:2; 14:28-33; 16:13-23; 17:1-9; 26:30-46; Jn 1:40-42; 18:10-11; 20:2-10; 21:1-21; Acts 1-15; Gal 1-2; 1, 2 Pt.

Pharaoh. Title of the kings of Egypt. At least ten are mentioned from the time of Abraham to the last king of Judah (Zedekiah); however, not all their names are known. The only sure names are from the later period, e.g., Neco (610-585 B.C.) who killed King Josiah of Judah, and Hophra (587-570 B.C.) who supported Zedekiah's rebellion against Nebuchadnezzar.
Gn 12:10-20; 39-50; Ex 5; 1 Kgs 9:16; 11; 2 Kgs 17:4; 19:9; 23:29-24:7; Jer 37:5; 44:30.

Philemon (loving). A friend of Paul who lived in Colossae and owned a slave, Onesimus.
See **Philemon, Epistle to,** sec. 1.

Philip (fond of horses). The name of eight men. (1) King of Macedon and father of Alexander the Great, who died in 336 B.C. (1 Mc 1:1). (2) The fifth king of Macedon to be called Philip who was defeated by the Romans in 197 B.C. (1 Mc 8:5). (3) Foster brother of Antiochus Epiphanes (1 Mc 6:14; 2 Mc 9:29). (4) Philip who was made governor of Judea by

Antiochus (2 Mc 5:22; 6:11). (5) Son of Herod the Great and first husband of Herodias (Mk 6:17). (6) Philip the Tetrarch, son of Herod the Great and Cleopatra (Lk 3:1). (7) Philip the apostle, who came from Bethsaida. At the Last Supper he asked Jesus to show them the Father (Mt 10:3; Jn 1:43-46; 6:5-7; 12:21-22; 14:8-9; Acts 1:13). (8) Philip the evangelist. One of the seven men chosen to be "deacons," he later preached in Samaria and other places. He baptized the Ethiopian eunuch on the road to Gaza. His four daughters had the gift of prophecy (Acts 6:1-6; 8; 21:8-9).

Pilate. Pontius Pilate, fifth Roman procurator in Judea (A.D. 26-37) after the removal of Archelaus in A.D. 6. He formally condemned Jesus to death.
Mt 27; Mk 15; Lk 3:1; 13:1; 23; Jn 18-19.

Rachel (ewe). An Aramean woman, daughter of Laban, and wife of Jacob. She became mother of Joseph and Benjamin.
Gn 29-30; 35:18-20.

Rahab. The name of a woman and a female monster. (1) A harlot who lived in a house in the walls of ancient (Bronze Age) Jericho. When two Israelite spies needed protection, she helped them and ensured they were not caught. Later when Jericho fell to Joshua's army, Rahab was allowed to join the Israelite people. The NT presents her as an example of true faith (Jos 2:6,17; 22:25; 6:17,23,25; Heb 11:31; Mt 1:5). (2) The female mythical monster of chaos, closely associated with Leviathan. Also used of Egypt in a derisory manner (Jb 9:13; 26:12; 38:8-11; Is 30:7; Ps 87:4).

Raphael (God heals). An angel who plays a leading role in the Book of Tobit. He is one of the seven angels who enter the holy presence and offer to God the prayers of his covenant people. He also appears on earth in disguise as a man to help first Tobit and then Tobit and Sarah.
Tb 3:17; 5-6; 8-9; 11-12.

Rebekah. A native of Mesopotamia, she became the wife of Isaac and mother of Esau and Jacob.
Gn 24; 25:19-26:16; 27.

Rehoboam (expansion of the people). Third and last king of the united kingdom, founded by David, and first king of the southern kingdom of Judah (931-913 B.C.). Son of Solomon and Naamah. As king he made the mistake of following his father's policy towards the northern tribes; they did not want to be burdened and so rebelled and formed the northern kingdom of Israel under Jeroboam.
1 Kgs 11:43-14:31; 2 Chr 9:31-13:7; Mt 1:7.

Ruth. The girl from Moab, who accompanied her mother-in-law, Naomi, to Bethlehem and there married Boaz. Through her son, Obed, she became an ancestress of King David.
See **Ruth, Book of,** sec. 1.

Salome (peace). The name of two women. (1) The wife of Zebedee and mother of James and John. She witnessed the crucifixion of Jesus and visited his tomb (Mt 27:56; Mk 15:40; 16:1). (2) The daughter of Herodias who danced before Herod the Tetrarch and received the head of John the Baptist (Mt 14:3-11; Mk 6:17-28).

Samson (little sun). A judge in Israel, known for his great strength. From birth he was dedicated to God as a Nazirite. Single-handedly he took on the Philistines; he gave away the secret of his strength to Delilah, whom he had married.
Jgs 13-16.

Samuel (the name of God). The earliest of the great Hebrew prophets and the last of the charismatic leaders (judges) in Israel. He was dedicated to the service of God by his mother, Hannah, and assisted the high priest, Eli, at the sanctuary in Shiloh until the latter's death.
1 Sm 1-4; 7-16; 18-24; 25:1.

Sarah (princess). Wife of Abraham and mother of Isaac, her original name of Sarai (an archaic word for princess) was changed to Sarah when she received God's promise that she would bear a son.
Gn 11-12; 16:1-18:15; 20-21.

Saul (asked of God). The name of three men. (1) A king of Edom (Gn 36:37-38). (2) The first king of Israel. Reckoned to be the tallest and handsomest man in Israel, as well as a great warrior, he was anointed king by Samuel. However, his rule, which began well, deteriorated and Samuel told him that God had chosen David as king instead. He was killed in battle against the Philistines along with his son, Jonathan (1 Sm 8-31; 2 Sm 1). (3) Original name of the apostle Paul (Acts 7:58; 13:9).
See **Paul,** sec. 2.

Sennacherib. King of Assyria 705-681 B.C. He attacked Jerusalem but was unable to capture it.
2 Kgs 18-19; 2 Chr 32; Is 36-37.

Shem. Eldest son of Noah and ancestor of the Semitic peoples.
Gn 6:9-10; 10:21-23.

Silas (or Silvanus). A leading member of the church in Jerusalem who possessed prophetical gifts. He was sent to Antioch to welcome Gentiles into the church. From here he went with the apostle Paul on his second missionary journey, and he shared imprisonment with him at Philippi.
Acts 15:22-41; 16; 17:1-15; 18:5; 2 Cor 1:19; 1 Thes 1:1; 2 Thes 1:1.

Simeon (God has heard). The name of six men. (1) The second son of Jacob and Leah, who became the ancestor of the tribe called Simeon (Gn 29:33; 46:10; 49:5-7; Nm 26:12-14). (2) An ancestor of Christ who lived after David (Lk 3:30). (3) A priest who was an ancestor of the Maccabees (1 Mc 2:1). (4) A righteous and devout man who knew that he would not die until he had seen the Messiah (Lk 2:25-35). (5) Simon Peter (Acts 15:14). (6) A Christian prophet at Antioch who was surnamed Niger (Acts 13:1).

Simon (Gk. form of "Simeon"). There are twelve men of this name. (1) Simon II, high priest, who is celebrated in Sir 50:1-21. (2) A Benjaminite who was captain of the temple guard (2 Mc 3:4-6; 4:1-6). (3) Second son of the priest Mattathias, also called Thassi (1 Mc 2:3; 5:17, 20-23; 11:59; 12:33-34). (4) Father of Judas Iscariot (Jn 6:71; 13:26). (5) Simon Peter, apostle (see **Peter,** sec. 2.). (6) Simon the Zealot, one of the twelve apostles (Lk 6:15; Acts 1:13). (7) One of the relatives of Jesus (Mt 13:55; Mk 6:3). (8) A Pharisee, at whose house Jesus ate (Lk 7:36-50). (9) A former leper who had a house in Bethany (Mt 26:6-13; Mk 14:3-9). (10) The Cyrenian who was compelled to carry the cross of Jesus (Mt 27:32). (11) A magician or sorcerer of Samaria (Acts 8:9-24). (12) A tanner of Joppa in whose house Peter stayed (Acts 9:43; 10:6).

Stephen (crown). The first Christian martyr. One of the seven deacons, he faithfully proclaimed Christ and was arrested. The supreme Jewish Council condemned him to death by stoning. Saul (Paul) watched this act.
Acts 6-7.

Susanna. Heroine of the story in chapter 13 of the Book of Daniel, but found only in the Greek version. Wife of Joakim, she refused to submit to the lustful desires of two corrupt elders. In revenge, they accused her of adultery and she was condemned to death. Daniel, however, recognized her innocence and the two men were themselves condemned and executed.
Dn 13:2-63.

Tamar (palm). The name of three women. (1) Wife, first of Er, eldest son of Judah and then also of Onan. After the latter's death, she seduced Judah himself and so he fathered her twins, Perez and Zerah (Gn 38:6ff; 1 Chr 2:4). (2) Daughter of David and Maacah. She was violated by Amnon her half-brother and then avenged by Absalom (2 Sm 13:1ff; 1 Chr 3:9). (3) Daughter of Absalom, named after her aunt and, like her, famed for her beauty (2 Sm 14:27).

Thomas (twin). One of the twelve apostles. According to tradition he was a missionary in Parthia, Persia, and India. Jn 11:16; 14:5-7; 20:24-29; 21:1-14; Acts 1:12-14.

Timothy (worshiping God). Companion and assistant of Paul. His mother was a Jewish Christian, his father a Greek. Two letters from Paul to him are in the NT.
Acts 16:1-3; 17:13-15; 1 Cor 4:17; 1 Thes 1:1; 3:1-6; 1, 2 Tm.
See **Timothy, Epistles of,** sec. 1.

Titus. The names of three men. (1) Titus Manius, Roman legate (2 Mc 11:34); (2) Titus Justus, a God-fearing Gentile (Acts 18:7); (3) a trusted companion of Paul. Although he is not mentioned in the Acts, a letter to him is found in the NT. The latter reveals that he labored in Crete (1 Cor 16:10; 2 Cor 2:13; 7:13-8:24; 12:18; Gal 2:1-3; 2 Tm 4:10, See **Titus, Epistle to,** sec. 1.

Tobit, Tobias (Gk. forms of Heb. Tobiah). In the Book of Tobit, the name "Tobit" is used of the father and "Tobias" (sometimes Tobiah) of the son. Tobit was deported from Israel to Nineveh in 721 B.C. After experiencing many misfortunes and becoming blind, he implored the Lord to let him die. At the same time he sent his son, Tobias, to Media to recover money he had deposited there. Accompanying and protecting the son was Raphael, an angel in disguise. Tobias not only regained the money but also married a woman named Sarah. On returning to his father with the money, his wife, and some medicine made from a fish, he rubbed the latter on his father's eyes and he was able to see again.

See **Tobit, Book of,** sec. 1.

Uriah (Yahweh is my light). Four men bear this name. (1) A Hittite who was one of David's mighty warriors. David committed adultery with his wife and then caused Uriah to be placed in such a vulnerable position in battle that he was killed (2 Sm 11-12; 1 Chr 11:41; Mt 1:6). (2) A priest (2 Kgs 16:10-16). (3) A prophet (Jer 26:20-24). (4) The father of Meremoth (Ez 8:33).

Zadok (righteous). A priest at king David's court. He had charge of the ark and took part in the anointing of Solomon as David's successor. He and his descendants acted as chief priests in Solomon's Temple until its destruction in 587 B.C.
2 Sm 15:24f; 1 Kgs 1:7ff.

Zechariah (Yahweh has remembered). There are thirty-three men of this name. The four most important are: (1) Son of Jehoida; he lived in the reign of king Joash of Judah and was martyred because he faithfully proclaimed the judgment of the Lord upon apostasy (2 Chr 24:20-22; Lk 11:51). (2) A king of Israel and last ruler in the dynasty of Jehu (2 Kgs 14:29; 15:8-12). (3) A prophet and priest who was born in the Exile in Babylon. He was a contemporary of Zerubbabel and Haggai and prophesied about 520 B.C. (See **Zechariah, Book of,** sec. 1). (4) The father of John the Baptist, husband of Elizabeth (Lk 1).

Zephaniah (Yahweh has hidden). The name of four men, including the prophet responsible for the ninth book of the Minor Prophets.
1 Chr 6:36-38; 2 Kgs 25:18-21; Zec 6:10, 14. See **Zephaniah, Book of,** sec. 1.

Zerubbabel (see of Babylon). Grandson of king Jehoiachin of Judah, he led exiles from Babylon to Jerusalem in 537 B.C. He was appointed governor of Judea and had the task of rebuilding the Temple, a task finished in 515 B.C.
Ezr 2:2; 3-5; Hg; and Zec 4.

Zipporah. Daughter of Jethro, priest of Midian, and wife of Moses. Though she apparently opposed the circumcision of their second son, Gershom, she felt compelled to perform the duty herself when she knew that Moses' life was endangered by its not being performed.
Ex 2:21; 4:24-26; Ex 18:2.

THREE

Places, People, and Nations

Achaia. See **Greece,** sec. 3.

Alexandria. A seaport on the Nile Delta in Egypt founded in 332 B.C. by Alexander the Great. It became a great center of trade and culture. The Greek version of the OT known as the Septuagint was translated here. It was the home of Apollos, an early Christian teacher.
Acts 6:9; 18:24; 27:6; 28:11.

Amalekites. Nomadic Arabian tribe, descendants of Amalek, who lived in the desert south of Judah. They opposed the Israelites in the days of Moses, Gideon, Samuel, David, and Hezekiah.
Ex 17:8; Jgs 7:12; 1 Sm 14:48; 27:8; 1 Chr 4:43.

Ammon, Ammonites. Descendants of Ben-ammi, Lot's younger son by his daughter. Therefore they were to be treated as relatives by the Israelites. In fact, they proved chronic enemies, oppressing Israel. They were defeated by the judge, Jephthah, by Saul, and by David. However, they later assassinated king Joash. The prophets denounced their constant antagonism, and Nehemiah protested about marriages between Jews and Ammonites. They lived east of the Jordan and their capital was Rabbah.

Gn 19:38; Dt 2:19; Jgs 3:13; 10:7, 11; 1 Sm 11:11; 2 Sm 10; Jer 49:1; Ez 25:1; Am 1:13; Zep 2:8; Ezr 9:1; Neh 13:23.

Amorites. Hill people, descendants of Canaan, who were to be dispossessed by the Israelites in their occupation of the promised land. Joshua overthrew the Amorite kings, Sihon and Og, and their territory was given to Israelites. The Amorites were gradually absorbed, but memories of their idolatry lingered.
Gn 10:16; Ex 33:2; Nm 13:29; 32:33; Dt 20:17; Jos 12:1-3; 1 Kgs 9:20; 21:26; 2 Kgs 21:11.

Antioch. Sixteen cities of this name were founded by Seleucus I Nicator (312-280 B.C.) in honor of his father. Two are mentioned in the NT. (1) Antioch of Pisidia in Phrygia, on the trade route between Ephesus and Cilicia. Paul visited there and was expelled. (2) Antioch on the Orontes, 300 miles north of Jerusalem, capital of the Roman province of Syria. Here there was a strong church which was responsible for missionary outreach.
Acts 11:26; 13:1-3, 14, 50; 15:1-3, 30-41.

Aram. OT name for Syria and north Mesopotamia. The inhabitants were Arameans, speaking Aramaic, and were divided into several tribes, one of which became the Chaldeans. They were referred to as descendants of Shem and figure often in the OT narrative because the Hebrew patriarchs were related by marriage to them.
Gn 10:22-23; 25:20; 31:20; Dt 26:5; 1 Chr 1:17.

Armageddon (mountain of Megiddo). The battlefield where the kings of the whole world gather for war on the great day of God, according to Rv 16:16. The name is framed from Megiddo, the place where great battles took place in OT times: (1) the defeat of Sisera, (2) the defeat and death of Ahaziah, and (3) the defeat and death of Josiah. See Jgs 5; 2 Kgs 9; 2 Kgs 23; Zec 12:11. The historical associations were used by John, the writer of the book of Revelation, to supply

an appropriate name for the future sorrows and triumphs of God's elect people.
Jgs 5:19; 2 Kgs 9:27; 2 Kgs 23:29; 2 Chr 35:20-24.
See **Megiddo,** sec. 3.

Ashdod. One of five Philistine cities.
Jos 11:22; 1 Sm 5:1. See **Philistines,** sec. 3.

Ashkelon. One of the five Philistine cities.
Jos 13:3; Am 1:8. See **Philistines,** sec. 3.

Asia. Today the continent east of Europe and Africa. In the OT, "Asia" was used in a narrower sense for the kingdom of the Seleucidae. In the NT, "Asia" refers to the region of Asia Minor (modern Turkey) and to the Roman province that formed its western portion.
1 Mc 8:6; 11:13; Acts 2:9; 16:6; 19:10-27; 20:18; 1 Cor 16:19; Rv 1:4.

Assyria. Country of upper Mesopotamia lying between Syria, Babylonia, Armenia, and Persia. Assur, Nineveh, and Calah were the chief cities. Assyria's power reached its peak during the seventh and eighth centuries B.C. Kings mentioned in the OT are Tiglath-pileser III (744-727), Shalmaneser V (726-722), Sargon II (721-705), Sennacherib (704-681), Esarhaddon (681-669), and Assurbanipal (669-627). The empire fell in 612.
Gn 10:11; 2 Kgs 15:27-16:9; 18:7-8; 19; 2 Chr 33:11-13; Is 7:17-25; Na 3:7,18; Zep 2:13.

Athens. Self-governing Greek city linked to Rome by a special treaty. As the ancient capital of Attica (Greece), it had lost all its political grandeur but remained a center of culture and learning by the time that Paul visited it to speak on its famous hill, the Areopagus.
Acts 17:15-34; 18:1; 1 Thes 3:1.

Babylon. Political and religious capital of Babylonia, situated on the east bank of the river Euphrates and founded by

Nimrod. The greatest king of the first Babylonian kingdom, Hammurabi (1792-1750 B.C.), is famous for his code of criminal, civil, and commercial law, bearing some resemblances to Mosaic law. The Assyrian king, Sennacherib, sacked the city in 689. Rebuilt by Esarhaddon it withstood a long seige by Assurbanipal. Nebolulassar improved it (626 B.C.) and Nebuchadnezzar raised it to its peak of glory. The city finally fell to the Persian king, Cyrus, in 539 B.C. (In the NT Babylon is used as a code name for Rome.)
Gn 10:10; 2 Kgs 24:1; 25:7-13; 2 Chr 33:11; Is 14:4,22; 21:9; 47:1; Jer 50-51; 1 Pt 5:13; Rv 14:8; 16:19; 17:5; 18:2, 10, 21.

Beersheba. Famous for its wells, situated fifty miles southwest of Jerusalem, where in turn Abraham, Isaac, and Jacob settled. The phrase "from Dan to Beersheba" denotes the most northerly and southerly places in the land of Israel.
Gn 21:31; 22:19; 26:33; 28:10; Jgs 20:1; 1 Sm 3:20; 2 Chr 30:5.

Bethany. Village two miles from Jerusalem on the Jericho road, the home of Mary, Martha, and Lazarus, as well as of Simon the Leper. Jesus made this his base during the last week of his life. Also a place east of Jordan where John baptized.
Mt 26:6; 21:7; Jn 1:28; 11:1.

Bethel. Originally called Luz, twelve miles north of Jerusalem. Abraham sacrificed here; later as a Canaanite city it was taken by the tribe of Ephraim. The sanctuary here was chosen by Jeroboam I to rival Jerusalem; it was the center for a school of prophets in Elijah's day, denounced for idolatry by Hosea and Amos.
Gn 28:9; 12:8; Jos 12:16; 18:22; Jgs 1:22; 1 Chr 7:28; 1 Sm 7:16; 10:3; 1 Kgs 12:26-29; 2 Kgs 2:2; Hos 4:5; Am 3:14.

Bethlehem. The city in Judah, five miles south of Jerusalem; originally called Ephrath and the site of Rachel's tomb; also

home of Boaz and David and the place where the Messiah was born. Also a city in Zebulun, seven miles northwest of Nazareth.
Gn 35:19; 48:7; Ru 2:4; 1 Sm 16; Mi 5:1; Mt 2:1; Jn 7:42.

Bithynia. Roman province in northwest Asia Minor, administratively linked with Pontus to the east. Paul and Silas were not allowed to preach here, but evidently others did.
Acts 16:7; 1 Pt 1:1.

Caesarea. Mediterranean port, twenty-three miles south of Mount Carmel, lavishly built by Herod the Great in honor of the emperor Augustus; the Roman procurators of Judea had their headquarters here.
Acts 23:23-38; 25:1-4.

Caesarea Philippi. A city, earlier called Pancas, below Mount Hermon, beautified by Herod the Great and Philip the Tetrarch, who renamed it partly in honor of Augustus Caesar. The scene of Peter's confession of Christ.
Mt 16:13.

Calvary. Site of the Crucifixion outside the city wall: the Latinized version of *Golgotha,* an Aramaic word meaning "skull."
Lk 23:33; Mt 27:33; Mk 15:22; Jn 19:17.

Canaan. A Semitic people and their homeland, strictly on the south Palestine coast. However, the term can be applied to Palestine as a whole.
Gn 10:15-19; Nm 13:17, 29; Dt 1:7; Gn 12:5.

Capernaum. Town by the sea of Galilee, two miles west of the Jordan. Frontier post of the tetrarchies of Herod and Philip and a Roman military base. Home of Peter and Andrew and the "headquarters" of Jesus for the Galilean ministry. The local people were unresponsive to his preaching.
Mt 17:24; 8:5; Mk 1:29; Mt 4:13; Lk 4:23; 10:15.

Cappadocia. A Roman province in the east of Asia Minor. Jews from here were present on the feast of Pentecost and its Christians were recipients of Peter's first letter.
Acts 2:9; 1 Pt 1:1.

Carmel. (1) A town in Judah, eight miles south of Hebron. Home of Nabal and Abigail and Hezro. On Saul's route when he returned from defeating the Amalekites (Jos 15:55; 1 Sm 15:12; 25; 2 Sm 23:25). (2) Range of hills, stretching for thirty miles from the Bay of Acre to Dothan. Elijah challenged Jezebel's gods there (1 Kgs 18:19; Sg 7:6; Am 1:2; Na 1:4).

Chaldea. South Babylonia, the home of Abraham. The Chaldeans were a Semitic people, a subdivision of the Arameans.
Is 48:20; Dn 1:4; 2:10; 4:7; 5:7,11; Hb 1:6.

Chebar. Babylonian river by which Jews were exiled; the scene of Ezekiel's visions.
Ezek 1:1; 3:15, 23; 10:15; 43:3.

Cilicia. Part of southeastern Asia Minor. Tarsus, Paul's home town, was the leading city.
Act 6:9; 15:23, 41; 27:5; 21:39; 22:3; 23:34; Gal 1:21.

Colossae. A city in Phrygia in the Lycus valley (western Asia Minor), ten miles from Laodicea on the main road to the East. Members of the church here included Philemon, his slave Onesimus, and Epaphras.
Col 1:2; 4:9; 12; Phlm 1, 10. See **Colossians, Epistle of Paul to,** sec. 1.

Corinth. Busy commercial city on the central isthmus of Greece, capital of the Roman province of Achaia. Paul's stay of eighteen months, unusually long for him, occurred around A.D. 52. Two-thirds of this cosmopolitan city were slaves and its immorality was proverbial.
Acts 18. See **Corinthians, Epistles of Paul to,** sec. 1.

Damascus. Capital of Syria (or Aram) astride trading routes from Egypt and Arabia to the East. Continuously occupied from prehistoric times, it was captured by David and later by the Assyrians. Here Paul was converted to Christ.
2 Sm 8:5; 1 Kgs 11:24; 20:34; 2 Kgs 16:9; 1 Chr 18:5; Is 7:8; 17:1; Amos 1:5; Acts 9.

Dead Sea. Inland lake, forty-seven miles long and three to nine miles wide, fed by the Jordan. At 1293 feet below sea level, it is the lowest body of water in the world. With no outlet the water is lost only by evaporation. The density of minerals in the water makes it five times saltier than the sea, and no fish or plants live in it. Called also Sea of Arabah and Salt Sea.
Gn 14:3; Dt 4:49; Ez 47:8-12, 18.

Decapolis. From 63 B.C. a federation of ten cities, all but one east of the Jordan. Gerasa and Damascus are mentioned in the NT. Pella was the refuge to which Jewish Christians fled in the Jewish-Roman war of A.D. 70.
Mt 4:25; Mk 5:20; 7:31; 13:14; Acts 9:2.

Ebal, Mount. See **Gerizim,** sec. 3.

Eden, Garden of. Abode of Adam and Eve at their creation, but from which they were expelled on account of their sin. Its beauty was proverbial. Also called the garden of God and garden of the Lord.
Gn 2:8; 3:23; Ez 28:13; 31:8-9; 18; 36:35; Jl 2:3; Is 51:3.

Edom. The land, south of the Dead Sea, occupied by the descendants of Esau (Edom); formerly Seir.
Gn 25:30; 32:3f; Nm 20:18; Am 1:6; Mal 1:4.

Egypt. A country dating back to 4000 B.C., occupying the northeast corner of Africa, mainly desert except where watered by the Nile. The pyramids date from around 2650 B.C. The foreign Hyksos occupied the land about 1700 B.C., but the ruler retained the title of Pharaoh. The Joseph stories

in Genesis belong to this period. The Egyptians ousted the Hyksos about 1560 B.C. and all aliens became suspect. The next 500 years again saw the expansion of its empire to the river Euphrates. Then decline set in and the Hebrew prophets continually warned Israel not to rely on Egyptian help.
Ex 1:8; Is 30:2; Jer 2:18; Ez 30:6; Gn 12:10,14; Gn 37-50; Ex 1-15.

Ekron. One of the five Philistine cities.
1 Sm 4:11; 5:10; 7:14. See **Philistines,** sec. 3.

Elam. An ancient mountainous land to the east of Babylonia with its capital at Susa (Shushan). The conquering Assyrians deported some Elamites to Samaria and some Israelites to Elam in the period of the Israelite monarchy. Although they were not Semites, Jews went to live among them and some were in Jerusalem on the Day of Pentecost.
Gn 14:1; Is 11:11; 21:2; Jer 25:25; Ezr 4:9; Acts 2:9.

Ephesus. In NT time the major port in Roman Asia Minor; now six miles from the sea, due to silting by the river Cayster. Its great open-air theatre seated 25,000 and its magnificent temple to the goddess Artemis was famous. Paul visited in A.D. 52 and returned later, eventually putting Timothy in charge of the church there. The church in Ephesus is the first addressed in the seven letters of Revelation.
Acts 19; 1 Cor 16:8; 1 Tm 1:3; Rv 2:1-7.

Ethiopia. Not the modern state but part of the kingdom of Nubia, stretching from present-day Khartoum to Aswan; often called Cush after the original settlers. Ethiopian armies were defeated by Asa, supported Hezekiah against Sennacherib, conquered Egypt, were beaten at Carchemish in 605 B.C., and were defeated by the Persians.
Gn 10:6; 2 Chr 14:9-15; 2 Kgs 19:9; Is 37:9; Jer 46:2,9; Na 3:9; Est 1:1.

Euphrates. The largest river in west Asia, running 1250 miles to the Persian Gulf. It is mentioned throughout the Bible from Genesis to Revelation. The river of Dt 11:24.
Gn 2:14; Ex 23:31; Jer 2:18; Rv 9:14.

Galatia. Northern region of modern central Turkey, named after the Celtic inhabitants (invaders from Gaul). A Roman province included this area and some southern regions and was called Galatia. Paul wrote his epistle to either the northern or southern region.
See **Galatia, Epistle of Paul to,** sec. 1.

Galilee. The upland region in north Palestine, west of the Jordan and Sea of Galilee; the scene of Jesus' upbringing and early ministry, and of a later resurrection appearance.
Mt 28:16; Mk 1:9, 39.

Galilee, Sea of. A pear-shaped lake, thirteen miles long and eight miles wide, fed by the Jordan. Also known as the Sea of Chinnereth or Chinneroth, the Sea of Genessaret, and the Sea of Tiberias. With some twenty-eight varieties of fish, the waters supported a flourishing fishing industry. Due to the height of the surrounding hills, contrasts in temperature give rise to sudden, intense storms. The ministry of Jesus is associated with several towns on its shores.
Nm 34:11; Js 12:3; Mt 4:13; 8:27; 14:22, 34; Lk 5:1; 8:32; Jn 6:23; 21:1.

Gath. One of the five Philistine cities, the home of Goliath.
1 Sm 17:4. See **Philistines,** sec. 3.

Gaza. The most southerly of the five Philistine cities. The scene of one of Samson's exploits and his end.
Jgs 16. See **Philistines,** sec. 3.

Gerizim. One of the two mountains (the other is Ebal) overlooking Shechem and known as the mount of blessing. Jotham addressed the Shechemites from a ledge halfway up,

where acoustics are remarkable. It was the sacred mountain of the Samaritans.
Dt 11:29; 27:4,13; Jos 8:33; Jgs 9:7; Jn 4:20.
See **Samaritans,** sec. 4.

Gethsemane. An estate, at the foot of the Mount of Olives and to the east of Kidron, which witnessed the agony of Jesus before his Crucifixion. Gethsemane means "an oil-press."
Mt 26:36; Mk 14:32.

Gilead. Hilly area east of the Jordan, divided by the Jabbok into two parts: the southern part assigned to the tribe of Gad and the northern part to Manasseh. It was well suited for grazing flocks and herds and for growing the spice known as "balm of Gilead."
Dt 3:16-17; Nm 32; Jos 12:2; 13:24-31; Jer 8:22.

Gilgal. The name of several places but primarily of the site between Jericho and the river Jordan where the Israelites made their first encampment after crossing the Jordan. It became their headquarters for the subsequent conquest of Canaan as well as a holy place where sacrifice was offered to God.
Jos 4:19-24; 15:17; 1 Sm 7:6; 11:15; 13:4-15; 2 Sm 19:15, 40; 2 Kgs 2:1-4; Hos 4:15; 9:15; 12:11; Amos 4:4; 5:5.

Greece. In NT times "Greece" refers to the Roman province of Achaia, made up of the whole of the Peloponnesus, with continental Greece south of Illyricum, Epirus, and Thessaly. Corinth was the capital and the residence of the proconsul, who ruled it.
Acts 18:12,27; 19:21; Rom 15:26; 2 Cor 1:1; 9:2; 1 Thes 1:7-8.

Greek Empire. Alexander I (the Great), ruler of the whole of Greece, overthrew the Persian Empire. He followed up his conquests with the enthusiastic importation of the Greek language, culture, and civilization. When he died in 323 B.C.

his empire was divided among his generals. The Jews in Palestine found themselves between the Seleucid Empire in Syria and Mesopotamia and the Ptolemaic Empire of Egypt for 250 years. The persecutions of the Maccabean period were due to the policy of Hellenization (enforcement of Greek ideas, values, and culture). In the century before Christ the Roman Empire replaced the Greek Empires.
1, 2 Mc.

Haran (Harran). A city of Mesopotamia by the river Balih; a commercial center on the main trade route between Babylonia and the Mediterranean. Abraham and Terah, as well as Jacob, lived here and it was the home of Rebekah.
Gn 11:31-32; 12:4-5; 8:10; 29:4-5; 2 Kgs 19:12; Is 37:12; Ez 27:23.

Hebron. The highest town in Palestine. Abraham lived nearby and his family was buried in the field of Machpelah nearby. During the conquest of the land by the Israelites, Hebron was taken by Caleb and given to his family. It was in this town that David was anointed king and it became, in the period of the monarchy, an important administrative center. After the Babylonian exile Jews returned to it but it was burnt by the Romans in the war A.D. 66-70.
Gn 23; 29:31; 50:13; Nm 13:22; Jos 14:12ff; 15:13-14; 2 Sm 2:4; 5:3; Neh 11:25; 1 Mc 5:65.

Hermon. The highest mountain (over 9,000 ft.) in the Anti-Lebanon range, also called Sirion and Senir (Shenir). It constituted the northeastern limit of the Israelite conquests under Joshua. It is possible that the Transfiguration occurred on its slopes.
Dt 3:8-9; Jos 11:3, 17; 12:1; Ps 42:6; 133:3; Mt 17:1

Hittites. An Indo-European race who controlled eastern Turkey and Syria from about 1600 to 1200 B.C. and whose capital city was Hattusha (near Ankara). The latter has recently been excavated, providing valuable information.

When this Empire collapsed, various outposts continued in northern Syria but most of the Hittites intermarried with other local peoples.
Gn 23; Jos 1:4; 1 Kgs 10:29-11:1; 2 Kgs 7:6.

Hivites, Horites, and Hurrians. A people known to us from 2500 B.C. who lived in the Fertile Crescent of Babylonia and became a part of the Hittite Empire.
Gn 14:6; 34:2; Jos 9:3-7.

Israel, Israelites. Originally the new name of Jacob, it was applied later to the whole body of his descendants ("house of Israel," "sons of Israel") and more particularly of the ten tribes which constituted the kingdom of Israel after the schism led by Jeroboam. The land of Israel "from Dan to Beersheba" was small, less than 150 miles in length and never more than 50 miles in width. The kingdom of Israel (in contrast to that of Judah) had two-thirds of the land in the north and had two shrines, one at Dan and another at Bethel, with the capital at Samaria. This kingdom fell to the Assyrians in 721 B.C. and a large number of people were carried away into Assyria.
Ex 32:4; Dt 4:1; 27:9; 2 Chr 11:13-14; 2 Kgs 17:7-8, 15; Hos 2:13; 4:2, 11, 15; Am 2:6-9. See also **Judah, Samaria,** sec. 3.

Jabbok. A tributary of the Jordan flowing from the east, rising near modern Amman and called now the Wadi Zerqa.
Gn 32:22; Nm 21:21f; Dt 3:16.

Jericho. This "city of palm trees," 820 feet below sea level and 17 miles east of Jerusalem, has had a continuous history from c. 8000 B.C., making it one of the world's oldest cities. However, the actual site of the city changed in late OT times so that the Jericho Jesus visited was not on the same site as that which Joshua beseiged and captured. It is first mentioned in the Bible with reference to the capture of Canaan by the Israelites under Joshua. By that time it had already been built and rebuilt many times. Herod the Great made it

important because of his building in and near Jericho. It was the city as restored by Herod that Jesus visited.
Dt 34:1,3; Jgs 3:13; Jos 5:13-6:27; 2 Kgs 2:5; 25:5; Ezr 2:34; Neh 7:36; 1 Mc 9:50; Mt 20:29; Lk 18:35; 19:1-2.

Jerusalem. In the tenth century B.C. this Jebusite (Canaanite) city high in the hills of Judah (at 2500 ft) was taken by David to become the capital and holy city of the Jews. His son, Solomon, made it a great city through his building program, including a temple, a palace, and walls. During the period of the divided monarchy, Jerusalem was the capital of Judah only. It was attacked several times and eventually fell to king Nebuchadnezzar in 586 B.C., when the city was laid waste and the Temple destroyed. Many Jews were taken away into captivity.

In 538 B.C. a group of exiles returned and laid the foundation of a new Temple; later the walls of the city were rebuilt by Nehemiah. At this time Jerusalem was in the Persian Empire. Later, in the period of the Greek empires, it once more experienced war and desolation. In 170 B.C. the Temple was desecrated by Antiochus Epiphanes, but it was soon recaptured and purified by the Maccabees. Then came the Roman Empire and under its rule, Herod the Great was able to make Jerusalem into a splendid city once again, with a rebuilt Temple. This was the Jerusalem which Jesus knew; it lasted until A.D. 70 when the Romans destroyed it and the Temple. Christianity began in Jerusalem and spread throughout the Roman Empire.
Gn 14:18; Jos 15:63; 2 Sm 5; 1 Kgs 6; 14:25-26; 2 Kgs 12:18; 18:13-19:36; 25; Ezr 5; Neh 3-6; Ps 48; 122; 1 Mc 4; Lk 2; 19:28-49; Acts 2; 15.

Jordan. The most important river in Palestine and thus intimately associated with the origins and history of both Judaism and Christianity. Rising twelve miles north of Lake Huleh it flows through this lake and the Sea of Galilee, then down to the Dead Sea. The straight-line distance is just over

100 miles, but because of its meandering its actual length is over 200 miles. Further, for most of its course it is below sea level. The Israelite tribes had to cross this river to begin their conquest of Canaan. John the Baptist called Jews, including Jesus, to this river for baptism.
Jos 3:1-17; 4:1-24; 2 Kgs 5:14; Mt 3:6,17.

Judah, kingdom of. The territory of the tribe of Judah and Benjamin including the people who remained faithful to the Davidic line at the division of the monarchy after Solomon's death. It was situated in southern Palestine with Jerusalem as capital and lasted from about 931 to 586 B.C., having nineteen kings of David's line. Because of false worship in the northern kingdom of Israel, not a few immigrants came south to Judah. As a small nation it had Egypt as a powerful neighbor in the southwest, and during the eighth and seventh centuries it had to reckon with the power of Assyria. From 605 B.C. the Babylonians under Nebuchadnezzar sought to subjugate Judah; its collapse occured in 586 B.C. After the Exile in Babylon, a weak Judah (also called Judea) existed under the Persian, Greek, Ptolemaic, Seleucid, and Roman rule with some independence under the Maccabees.
1 Kgs 12; 2 Kgs 25; Ez-Neh; 1, 2 Mc.

Judea. The Greek and Roman name for Judah, usually referring to the southern part of Palestine.

Kadesh-barnea. An oasis containing a spring of water that flows all year, situated at the southern end of Palestine. Abraham lived here for a time and the Hebrews in their desert wanderings twice encamped here.
Gn 14:7; 16:14; Nm 20:13f; 33:36; Dt 1:19-25; Jos 10:41; 15:23.

Kidron (Cedron). A valley between the eastern wall of Jerusalem and the Mount of Olives. It may be followed all the way from there to the Dead Sea. Those who travel from

the city to Bethany and Jericho must cross it; water is found there only after heavy rain.
2 Sm 15:23; 1 Kgs 15:13; 2 Chr 29:16; 23:4; Jn 18:1.

Lachish. A fortified city covering eighteen acres in the lowland of southern Palestine, thirty miles southwest of Jerusalem. Its king was defeated by Joshua in the Hebrew conquest of Palestine. Later, as a city of the kingdom of Judah, it was besieged first by Sennacherib of Assyria and then by Nebuchadnezzar of Babylon and was destroyed. It was later reoccupied and came near to its former size and influence. Important archaeological discoveries have been made here.
Jos 10:3-35; 12:11; 2 Kgs 14:19; Kgs 18:14,17; 19:18; 14:10-25:20; 2 Chr 11:9; 25:27; Neh 11:30.

Lebanon. The name of a snow-clad mountain range in Syria as well as of the fertile area between it and the Mediterranean. The mountains had forests of large cedars, and also firs and cypresses. The wood was used for building houses and palaces as well as ships. The Phoenician ports of Tyre, Sidon, and Byblos prospered through exporting the wood and produce of this area.
Jer 18:14; 1 Kgs 5:6-10; 2 Kgs 19:23; Ps 72:6; Is 2:13; 14:8; Ez 31.

Macedonia. A country north of Greece which came into prominence and then world dominion under Philip (359-336 B.C.) and Alexander the Great (336-323 B.C.). In 168 B.C. it fell to the Romans and became a Roman province in 148 B.C.: the cities of Philippi, Beroea, and Thessalonica were part of it. Paul, Silas, and Timothy evangelized here.
Acts 16:8-17:15; 20:1-6; 2 Cor 8:1-5; 9:1-5; Phil 4:15; 1, 2 Thes.

Media. A country in Asia, now northwest Iran; inhabitants known as Medes. Israelites were transported to the cities of

Media when Samaria fell to the Assyrians in 721 B.C. The empire of the Medes gave way to that of the Persians. Later it was the Medes and the Persians who overthrew the Babylonian Empire.
2 Kgs 17:6; 18:11; Is 13:17; 21:2,9; Jer 51:11,28; Dan 5:28; 8:20; Acts 2:9.

Megiddo. An important Palestinian city, captured by Joshua from the Canaanites. It was strategically important, commanding the pass through the mountains between the Plains of Sharon and Esdraelon. Solomon extended and fortified it. Excavations have revealed stables for 450 horses. It was the scene of great battles, e.g., between Pharaoh Neco and king Josiah.
Jos 12:21; 1 Kgs 9:15,19; 10:26; 2 Kgs 23:29; 2 Chr 35:22; Rv 16:16.
See also **Armageddon,** sec. 3.

Mesopotamia. A Greek name appearing after the time of Alexander the Great and referring to the whole area between the rivers Euphrates and Tigris. The older name was Aram.
Jdt 2:24; 5:7-8; 8:26; Acts 2:9; 7:2.

Midian. A region in Arabia near the Gulf of Aqaba and bordered on the northwest by Edom. Moses married a Midianite woman; later the Israelites and Midianites were enemies.
Gn 25:2-4; Ex 2:15-22; Nm 22:4; 25:1,6; Jos 13:21; Jgs 6:1-40; 8:5, 10-11.

Moab. The region east of the Dead Sea with the northern border at the Arnon inhabited by the descendants of Moab, Lot's son. It was a rolling plateau, some 3,200 feet above sea level. Originally the country included what were called "the Plains of Moab," the area east of the Jordan opposite Jericho. The Moabites became a settled people before the Israelites settled in Canaan and were often at war with them.
Gn 19:37-38; Nm 21:11-13; Jgs 3:12-30; 1 Sm 14:47; 2 Sm

8:2,12; 1 Chr 8:2,11; 2 Kgs 13:20; 24:2; Is 15; 16; Jer 48; Am 2:1-2.

Nabateans. An Arabian tribe who settled in the former territory of Edom and Moab by the fourth century B.C., the capital of which was Petra. The civilization prospered through their own ingenuity in the use of the land and also through imposing duties on the goods passing along the trade routes through the land. They managed to remain independent of Rome with their own line of kings until A.D. 106.
1 Mc 5:25; 9:35.

Nazareth. Not mentioned in the OT, it was the town in Galilee, eighty-eight miles north of Jerusalem, where Mary and Joseph lived and where Jesus was brought up. However, in the period of his public ministry, the townspeople rejected him.
Mt 2:23; 4:13; 13:54-58; Mk 6:1-6; Lk 2:39; 4:28-32.

Nineveh. An ancient city on the east bank of the river Tigris at the mouth of a small tributary known as the Khoser. Its deity was the goddess Ishtar and her temple there dated from c. 2400 B.C. Under king Sennacherib it became the capital of Assyria (from c. 700 B.C.) and to it the Assyrians brought the spoils of war. King Assurbanipal gathered a magnificent library there around 650 B.C. The city was totally destroyed by the Medes in 612 B.C.
Gn 10:11-12; Jon 1:2; 3:3; Jdt 1:1; 2 Kgs 19:36; Na 1-3; Zep 2:13-15.

Olives, Mount of. A hill to the east of Jerusalem, separated from the city by the Valley of Kidron. David went up this mountain while fleeing from Absalom, Ezekiel had a vision there, and Jesus often went up and down it.
2 Sm 15:14; Ez 11:23; Zec 14:4; Mt 21:1; 26:30; Lk 21:37; 22:39; Jn 8:1; Acts 1:12.

Persia. In a general sense Persia was the land with boundaries at the Persian Gulf, the valley of the Tigris, the Caspian Sea and the rivers Oxus, Jaxartes, and Indus. The Persian Empire, which replaced that of the Babylonians and Medes and was itself replaced by that of Alexander the Great, stretched from India to Greece. Persians were Aryan people, closely related to the Medes; their religion was Zoroastrianism. They are only mentioned in the later books of the OT; it was their king Cyrus the Great who was responsible for the resettlement of Jerusalem from 538 B.C.
2 Chr 36:22-23; Ezr 1; 4; Est 10:2; 1 Mc 3:31; 6; Dn 10.

Philippi. A city in Macedonia, located eight miles from the sea and named after its founder, Philip II of Macedon. It became part of the Roman Empire in 167 B.C. and after 42 B.C. was a Roman colony, subject to Roman law. Paul and Silas visited on the first missionary journey and founded the first church in Europe there. Later Paul revisited and wrote a letter to the young church.
Acts 16:6-40; 20:6; Phil 1:1; 1 Thes 2:2. See **Philippians, Epistle to,** sec. 1.

Philistines. A people from southwestern Asia Minor who reached Palestine via Crete by the twelfth century B.C. They introduced iron into the region but also adopted Canaanite culture and religion. Their gods—Dagon and Baal-zebub—bear Semitic names. The five fortified cities of Gaza, Ashkelon, Ashdod, Ekron, and Gath were the major centers from which they conducted warfare over eight centuries against the Israelites. By NT times they seem to have disappeared as a separate people.
Jgs 13-16; 1 Sm 4-6; 13:19-22; 1 Kgs 5:1; 2 Kgs 18:8; 1 Mc 5:66-68.

Phoenicia. The narrow coastal strip of 250 miles from Mount Carmel to Jebel Akron (Mount Casius) between the Lebanon range and the Mediterranean Sea; its chief city-states were Tyre and Sidon. Its inhabitants, the Phoenicians,

were a Semitic people with a religion like that of the Canaanites. They were heavily involved in trade and commerce in the Mediterranean. Jesus visited this area.
2 Mc 3:5-8; Mt 15:21; Mk 7:24-31; Acts 11:19; 15:3; 21:2-3.

Pithom. A city in Egypt on whose construction the Hebrew slaves worked. It was used as a store-city.
Ex 1:11.

Rameses. A city in Egypt, named after Pharaoh Rameses II, on which the Hebrew slaves worked. It was also the place from where they began their journey to the promised land (Canaan).
Ex 1:11; 12:37; Nm 33:3,5.

Red Sea. This expression is used both of (1) that sea which today is called the Red Sea (between the continent of Africa and the peninsula of Arabia) and (2) the "sea of reeds," a lake in the area where the Suez canal is now found (and the original lakes drained). In the Exodus the Israelites probably crossed (2).
(1) Nm 14:25; 21:4; Dt 1:40; 2:1; 1 Kgs 9:2; 2 Chr 8:17; (2) Ex 10:19; 15:4,22; Nm 33:10f; Dt 11:4.

Roman Empire. The birth and crucifixion of Jesus Christ took place under Roman rule for Judea had been subject to Rome since 63 B.C. That rule was exercised in Palestine through the appointment of local kings (e.g., Herod) or officials from Rome (e.g., Pilate). The Christian church was able to expand quickly because Roman peace, roads, and security, as well as the general use of the Greek language (inherited from the previous Greek Empire) extended throughout the Mediterranean world. It had a strong center in Rome itself. However, the arrogance of Roman imperialism posed a threat to the confession of Christ as Lord in the later NT period.
1 Mc 8; Jn 11:48; Acts 28:17-18; Rom 1:15; 1 Pt 2:13 cf Rv 17:6, 14.

Samaria. Used in three ways. (1) As the capital of the kingdom of Israel from the time of king Omri, its builder, to its fall to the Assyrians in 721 B.C. It was often a center for idolatry and was promised divine judgment by various prophets. It was rebuilt by Herod the Great (1 Kgs 16:24; 2 Kgs 17:3-6; Is 7:9; 8:4). (2) The territory occupied by the ten tribes of the kingdom of Israel (1 Kgs 13:32; 2 Kgs 17:24). (3) A district in central Palestine under Roman administration (Lk 17:11; Jn 4:4; Acts 8:5).
See **Samaritans,** sec. 4.

Shechem. An important city in central Palestine visited by the patriarchs. After the Israelite conquest of Canaan, Joshua supervised the renewal of the covenant with the Lord there. It became a city of refuge and a levitical city. After Solomon's death, the assembly of Israel made Jeroboam king here, and it served for a short time as the capital of the kingdom of Israel. After the Babylonian Exile, Shechem was the chief city of the Samaritans and in the Greek period (c. 300-100 B.C.) it was a thriving city.
Gn 12:6-7; 33:18-19; 34:25-26; 35:1-4; Jos 8:30-35; 24; 20:7; 21:21; 1 Kgs 12:1-19; 1 Chr 6:67.

Shiloh. A town in the central Palestine mountain range. Here, in the period after the Conquest the Tabernacle was kept and the people assembled as the tribes of the Lord. However, c. 1050 B.C. the Philistines captured the Ark of the covenant and destroyed the city, an event interpreted as God's judgment.
Jos 18:1-10; 22:9-12; Jgs 18:3; 21:19-21; 1 Sm 1-4; Ps 78:60; Jer 7:12, 14.

Sinai. The mountain (also called Horeb) at which the Hebrews arrived after crossing the Red Sea and journeying for three months from Egypt. From this mountain God gave his Law to Moses and at its base the covenant between the Lord and the Israelites was made. The precise location is not

certain but probably in the area now called the Sinai Peninsula.
Ex 19:1-2; 20:1-24:8; 1 Kgs 19:8; Acts 7:30,38.

Sodom. One of the five cities in the Plain of the Jordan, chosen by Lot as his residence. With other cities it was destroyed, but Lot and his two daughters were spared. The name became a symbol for organized wickedness.
Gn 13:10-13; 14:11, 17-24; 19:1-19; Dt 29:23; Is 1:9-10; Mt 10:15; 11:24; 2 Pt 2:6; Jude 7; Rv 11:8.

Syria. Abbreviation of Assyria and the name of the most important province in the Greek kingdom of the Seleucids. In 64 B.C. this became a Roman province, designating the part of western Asia with boundaries at the Taurus Mountains in the north, the Euphrates in the east, Palestine in the south, and the Mediterranean in the west
1 Mc 11:2,60; Mt 4:24; Lk 2:2; Acts 15:23,41; 18:18; 20:3; 21:3; Gal 1:21.

Thessalonica. Named after Thessalonike, sister of Alexander the Great, and founded as Macedonia became the center of a great empire. It became the principal metropolis of Macedonia, being situated on the great trade routes from Italy to the East and from the Aegean to the Danube. Paul evangelized here and wrote two letters to the church he founded.
Acts 17:1-9; 1, 2 Thes.

Tigris. Also called Hiddekel, this river of Mesopotamia is 1146 miles long, flowing from the Armenian mountains into the Euphrates and thence into the Persian Gulf. One of the four rivers marking the location of the Garden of Eden.
Gn 2:14; Dn 10:4; Tb 6:1.

Ur of the Chaldees. The city on the banks of the Euphrates which Terah and Abraham left to go to Haran, beginning the patriarchal pilgrimage. Excavations have revealed a rich civilization there.
Gn 11:28,31; 15:7; Neh 9:7.

FOUR

Religion (Cults, Institutions, Parties)

Abomination of Desolation (or the horrible abomination, the desolating sacrilege). A phrase from the book of Daniel used to describe the action of Antiochus Epiphanes, who in 167 B.C. desecrated the Jerusalem Temple by installing an altar of Zeus. By this act the divine presence was withdrawn and true worship had to cease. Jesus warned of the repetition of such an event and Paul applied the phrase to Antichrist.
Dn 9:27; 11:31; 12:11; 1 Mc 1:54,59; 2 Mc 6:2; Mt 24:15; Lk 21:20; 2 Thes 2:3-4.

Altar. A place of meeting with God where the worshiper offered a gift of sacrifice. First mentioned after the Flood, altars were built of earth, unhewn stone, or wood overlaid with bronze in order to be fireproof. They were erected by Abram, Isaac, Jacob, Moses, Balaam, Elijah, David, Solomon, and Ahaz. Unlawful altars were condemned.
Gn 12:7; 26:25; 33:20; Ex 17:15; Nm 23:1; 1 Kgs 18:32; 2 Sm 24:25; 2 Chr 4:1; 2 Kgs 16:10.

Altar of burnt offering. A hollow, square altar made of acacia wood covered with bronze, with four bronze horns at the corners, placed in the outer court of the Tabernacle and Temple in order to be accessible. The fire on it was kept permanently lit.
Ex 27:1-8; 1 Kgs 8:64; 2 Chr 7:7.

Altar of incense. A square altar made of acacia wood and overlaid with gold and with horns of gold, for the burning of the holy incense.
Ex 30:1-10; Lev 2:2; 16; Lk 1:11.

Anointing. Consecrated oil was poured on to people and objects to signify their being set apart for God and his service. Thus places of worship, kings, priests, and prophets were anointed. Further, the action is associated with the gift of the Holy Spirit.
Ex 30:22f; 40:9f; 1 Sm 16:13; 2 Sm 2:4; 1 Kgs 19:16; Acts 10:38.

Ark, Noah's. Vessel of gopher wood, reeds, and bitumen, built according to divine instructions for the preservation of Noah and his family, together with a selection of animals, from the judgment of the Flood.
Gn 6-9; 1 Pt 3:20.

Ark of the covenant. Rectangular box of acacia wood, covered with gold. Its lid (mercy seat) was of solid gold, surmounted by two cherubim with outstretched wings. Details for its construction were divinely revealed to Moses and undertaken by Bezalel at Sinai. It contained the two tablets inscribed with the Ten Commandments, a pot of manna, and Aaron's rod. When Solomon's Temple was destroyed in 587 B.C. the ark was lost and thus there was no ark in the Second Temple. It had been kept in the inner sanctuary (the holy of holies).
Ex 25; 37:1; Lv 16:2.

Artemis. Greek goddess of the moon and of hunting (Diana to the Romans). Her temple at Ephesus was one of the seven wonders of the world. By tradition her image (probably a meteorite) fell out of the sky. When Paul's preaching threatened to bring a slump in the local trade in small votary shrines, the silversmiths staged a riot.
Acts 19:24f.

Ashtaroth. Canaanite mother-goddess of fertility, love, and war, especially prominent in Sidon: the depraved cult attracted the Israelites. Also the name of the capital city of Og, king of Bashan.
Dt 1:4; Jgs 2:13; 10:6; 1 Sm 7:3-4.

Astrologers. Astrologers are mentioned together with magicians and enchanters in the Book of Daniel and as students of the stars in Matthew's birth narrative.
Dn 2:27; 4:7; 5:7-11; Mt 2:1,7,16.

Atonement, Day of. Annual solemn fast on the tenth day of the seventh month (Tishri, September-October), reminding the Jews that the many daily, weekly, and monthly sacrifices of the Temple were insufficient to atone for sin. On this one day, the high priest, dressed in a simple white robe, entered the holy of holies (after both he and the sanctuary had been ceremonially cleansed). There he burnt incense and sprinkled blood on the mercy seat (lid of the Ark) to make atonement for the priesthood. Blood from a sacrificed goat was also sprinkled in the holy of holies, this time for the people. Further, he laid his hands upon a second, living goat, confessing over it the sins of Israel. This scapegoat was then driven into the wilderness, symbolizing the carrying away of their sins.
Lv 16; Heb 13:11-12.

Baal. OT term for Canaanite nature and fertility gods, led by Hadad, the storm god. The Baal challenged by Elijah on Mount Carmel was Melqart, god of Tyre. The Baal fertility cults constantly infected Israel's worship of their covenant God and brought strong condemnation from the prophets.
Jgs 6:25,28,30; 1 Kgs 18; Jer 7:9; Hos 2:10.

Baptism. The act of immersing a person in water, or pouring water over the head, as an act of cleansing or initiation. The Jews baptized Gentile converts to Judaism: John the Baptist caused a sensation by baptizing Jews, a

practice continued by Jesus and his disciples. In the church, at Jesus' command, baptism became the rite of union with Jesus himself and entry into the church.
See **Baptism, Christian,** sec. 6.

Bishop. The overseer of a church, equivalent in the NT to elder or presbyter.
Phil 1:1; 1 Tm 3:1; Ti 1:5,7.

Booths, Feast of. One of the three annual Jewish pilgrimage festivals, also called the feast of tabernacles and of ingathering. Sacrifices were offered on seven days (15-22 of the seventh month, Tishri) with a special celebration on the eighth day. While coinciding with the completion of harvest, the historic significance was a reminder of the nomad life after the deliverance from Egypt.
Lv 23:33f; Dt 16:13f; 2 Chr 8:13; Jn 7:2.

Burnt Offering. A sacrifice wholly burnt, except for the skin, to atone for sins. The victim had to be a clean animal, without blemish; sacrifices were offered daily.
Lv 1; 7:8; Nm 28-29.

Calf, golden. (1) The idolatrous image made by Aaron and the Israelites and then destroyed by Moses on his return from Mt. Sinai (Ex 32). (2) After the division of the kingdom, Jeroboam I set up two golden calves at Bethel and Dan, in Israel, as centers of worship to divert attention from the temple of Jerusalem in the kingdom of Judah. Hosea prophesied their destruction (1 Kgs 12:28; 2 Kgs 10:29; Hos 8:6).

Cereal Offering. A sacrifice of flour, baked cakes, or plain grain, with oil, frankincense, and salt, accompanied by wine. No leaven or honey was to be used. A portion was burnt at the altar and the rest went to the priests. In the case of the poor, it could replace a burnt offering.
Lv 2:1-16; 23:13; Nm 5:11f.

Chemosh. Moabite god: child sacrifice was practiced by his worshipers. Solomon's high place for Chemosh in Jerusalem was destroyed by Josiah.
Nm 21:29; 1 Kgs 11:7; 2 Kgs 3:27; 23:13; Jer 48:13.

Circumcision. The ancient custom of removing the foreskin, practiced in Israel and also in Egypt, Edom, Ammon, and Moab, but not among Assyrians, Babylonians, or Philistines. It symbolized covenant membership within a community. Carried out by Jews on the eighth day after birth, even if that were a sabbath: metaphorically it described loyalty to God. In the church, circumcision was not required of Gentiles.
Gn 17:10; Lv 12:3; Jn 7:22; Gal 2:3; 5:1-12; Col 2:11.

Clean and unclean. In Mosaic law, that which allowed or disqualified a worshiper from approaching God. Ceremonial defilement came by contact with a dead body or with leprosy, through certain bodily functions (e.g., menstruation), or through eating animals listed as unclean. Provision for cleansing was defined in each case.
Lev 10:10; 11-15; Nm 19:11; Dt 14.

Council of Jerusalem. The meeting in A.D. 45 between representatives from the church of Antioch, led by Barnabas and Paul, and the leaders of the church in Jerusalem to discuss problems arising from the increasing influx of Gentile converts to Christ.
Acts 15.

Deacon (Gk. *diakonos,* "servant") An order of ministry whose functions were not clearly defined in the NT period. One woman is called a deaconess.
Phil 1:1; 1 Tm 3:8-13; Acts 6:2-6; Rom 16:1.

Dedication, Feast of. An eight-day festival, originally to celebrate the winter solstice but later to commemorate the reconsecration of the Jerusalem Temple by Judas Maccabeus

in 164 B.C., exactly three years after its defilement by Antiochus Epiphanes. Also called the Feast of Lights from the special illuminations in private houses for the event.
1 Mc 1:54,59; 4:36-39; 2 Mc 2:9,18; 10:6; Jn 10:22,36.

Disciple. One who learns a way of life from another by following his teaching and especially by being in his company. Applied in particular to the Twelve, and used of followers of Jesus in the Acts. It is not, however, used in the Epistles.
Mt 10:1-2; Lk 9:57-62; Acts 6:1; 9:19.

Dispersion, The. Jews scattered in the Gentile world; used metaphorically of Christians scattered in this world.
Jn 7:35; Jas 1:1; 1 Pt 1:1.

Divination. The attempt to gain knowledge of events that are distant in time or space and which cannot be gained by usual or normal methods. Most forms of it are condemned in the Bible. The diviner may go into a trance or he may use mechanical means (sand, livers, sticks), he may have a dream, or he may consult the stars.
Ez 21:21; Dt 18:11; Lv 19:26; Acts 16:16. See also **Magic,** sec. 4.

Drink Offering (Libation). This accompanied the cereal-offering in the Temple to acknowledge God as the provider of basic food and drink.
Ex 29:38-42; Lv 23:13; Nm 8:10.

Elder. One in a community invested with authority on grounds of seniority of age or experience. The elders of Israel were influential both locally and nationally. The members of the Sanhedrin were called elders.

The local Christian churches were ruled by a group of elders, sometimes called bishops, on the Jewish model. Sometimes one elder was singled out as the "ruler."
Ex 3:16; 12:21; Nm 11:16; Acts 11:30; 14:23; 15:2-23; Ti 5:7; 1 Pt 5:1; 3 Jn 1. See **Bishop,** sec. 4.

Ephod. An upper garment worn by the high priest, being one of the six sacred vestments he was required to wear in worship. It was elaborate in color and design while that worn by ordinary priests was much simpler.
Ex 28:4-9; 1 Sm 22:18.

Epicureans. Philosophers who followed the teaching of Epicurus (341-270 B.C.). Paul came across Epicureans in Athens. They sought happiness through tranquil detachment.
Acts 17:18

Essenes. A Jewish sect not mentioned in the Bible which arose in the second century B.C. as a protest against both Greek influence in Judaism and carelessness in religious observance among Jews. It is possible that the writers of what we call the Dead Sea Scrolls were of this sect.
See **Dead Sea Scrolls,** sec. 1.

Evangelist. One called to proclaim the evangel, the good news of Jesus.
Acts 21:8; Eph 4:11; 2 Tm 4:5.

Fasting. Abstaining from food and drink for a religious purpose to express grief, penitence, devotion, and to seek guidance or help. There was an annual Jewish fast on the Day of Atonement and some Pharisees fasted twice weekly. Forty-day fasts are recorded for Moses, Elijah, and Jesus.
Mt 4:2; 6:16-17; 9:14-15.

Feasts, Festivals. The law of Moses required every male to attend at the sanctuary in Jerusalem at three annual feasts—*Passover,* (Unleavened Bread); *Weeks* (Harvest, Firstfruits, Pentecost); *Booths* (Tabernacles, Ingathering). Further there were the festivals of *Purim* and *Dedication,* which were later additions. The weekly *Sabbath,* the Day of the Blowing of *Trumpets* and the Day of *Atonement* were also seen as feasts to the Lord. Each feast is treated separately.

Firstborn. God had the prior claim to the firstborn of both animals and men, since he is Creator. Further, by the deliverance from the last plague in Egypt of the firstborn, God had established a special claim upon the firstborn in Israel.
Ex 12:12-13,23,29; 13:2,13,15; 34:19-20; Lv 27:26.

Freewill Offering. See **Peace Offering,** sec. 4.

Gentile. Name given by Jews for a non-Jew. The admission of Gentiles into the early church began with the conversion of Cornelius.
Acts 10:28,45; 11:18.

God-fearer. Name given by Jews to those Gentiles who attended the synagogue and observed some Jewish practices. They were not converts since they were not circumcised.
Acts 10:2,22; 13:16,26,43,50; 16:14; 17:4,17; 18:7. See **Proselyte,** sec. 4.

Guilt Offering. See **Sin and Guilt Offerings,** sec. 4.

Herodians. Jewish supporters of Herod Antipas, Tetrarch of Galilee and Perea from 4 B.C. They were usually also Sadducees and hostile to Jesus.
Mk 3:6; 12:13.

High Places. Localities, usually on the top of hills and near towns, used for the worship of a deity. The Canaanites used them; on entering Canaan the Israelites were told to destroy them. Later the prophets condemned the high places where Israelites joined in the worship of Baal.
Nm 33:52; Ez 6:3.

High Priest. The supreme representative of Israel before their God. His duties were the oversight of the Temple and its worship. He could offer sacrifices on any day but he had particular responsibility on the Day of Atonement, when he alone entered the holy of holies. He also presided over the

Sanhedrin. His special dress was: a square golden breastpiece; an embroidered ephod; the blue robe of the ephod, and the linen miter. He was set apart to the office by the pouring of oil upon his head and, although he was supposed to be in office for life, he could be removed by the civil authority.
Ex 29; Lv 4:3, 5, 16; 21:16, 23; 2 Kgs 12:7f; Mt 26:57; Acts 5:21.

Holocaust. See **Burnt Offering,** sec. 4.

Hymns. In the Jerusalem Temple psalms were sung; the Hebrew title of the Book of Psalms is "Songs of Praise," even though not all are actually poems of praise. Along with psalms of praise and thanksgiving there are psalms of lament and entrance liturgies. In the apostolic church not only psalms but also "spiritual songs" were sung, along with canticles and doxologies.
2 Chr 7:6; Neh 12:8; 1 Cor 14:15; 26; Lk 1:46-55; 68-79; 2:29-32; 1 Tm 6:15-16.

Idols. Both Israel and the early church faced a context in which idolatry was commonplace. Israel faced the religion of Canaan and the church that of the Roman Empire. In the preexilic period, the temptation for Israel was to capitulate to the use of graven and molten images, pillars, the asherah and teraphim: in other words to act as did the Canaanites. They knew that the second commandment forbade all such capitulation and that their God could not be represented by an idol.

After the Exile, the tendency to idolatry was halted and images were seen as deceitful and demonic. This was the position taken up by the apostles concerning the idolatry of the Greek and Roman cities.
Ex 20:2-5; Dt 4:15-24; Acts 17:29; Jgs 8:24-27; 17:1-18:31; Eph 5:5. See **Abomination of Desolation; Ashtaroth; Baal; Calf, golden; Chemosh; Pillar,** all in sec. 4.

Incense. Fragrant substances such as gums and spices burned in the ritual of Israelite worship. The Temple had an altar of incense on which each morning the high priest burned incense. The ingredients were equal proportions of stacte or opobalsamum, onycha, galbanum, and pure frankincense, tempered with salt. Incense symbolized the offering of prayer to God.
Ex 25:6; 30:1-10; 35:8, 28; 37:9; Nm 16:46-47; Ps 141:2; Lv 16:12-13.

Lampstand. In the Tabernacle there stood an elaborate golden lampstand with six branches and seven lights: Solomon's Temple had ten such lamps. They burned olive oil.
Ex 25:31-40; 37:23; 1 Kgs 7:49.

Levites. The descendants of Levi (son of Jacob) whose menfolk had the responsibility of the care of the Tabernacle and, later, of assisting the priests in the Temple. In David's reign they were divided into four classes: (1) assistants to the priests in the sanctuary; (2) judges and scribes; (3) gatekeepers; (4) musicians.
Ex 32:26-29; Nm 3:44f; 1 Chr 24-26; 2 Chr 11:13-15.

Libation. See **Drink Offering,** sec. 4.

Lord's Day. The first day of the week when Christians met to celebrate the Resurrection and for worship. Now called Sunday.
Rv 1:10.

Lord's Supper. The oldest name for what is the sacrificial, thanksgiving meal of Christians. It commemorates the atoning death of Christ.
1 Cor 11:20; Lk 22:19; Mt 26:28; Mk 14:24.

Lots. Stones or inscribed tablets were put into a vessel and, after being shaken, were drawn out or cast forth, after prayer

to God had been offered. Thus it was a way of God making known his will to his trusting people.
Jos 14:2; 18:6; Prv 16:33; Acts 1:23-26.

Magic. The strong prohibitions of the Law of Moses against magic and sorcery reveal how widespread they were, not only in Canaan but also in Egypt and Assyria. Magic was closely associated with religion and practiced by educated priests. Black magic sought to produce evil results through curses and spells while white magic sought to undo the effects of black magic or to use occult forces for the good of a person. Israel was often under pressure to adopt magic or sorcery; Jezebel practiced sorcery.
Lv 19:26; 20:27; Dt 18:10-14; Ex 7:11,22; 8:7,18-19; 2 Kgs 9:22; Ez 13:17-13; Acts 8:9,11.

Nazirite. A person specially consecrated to God either for life or for a limited period. No alcoholic drink could be taken and the hair must not be cut. Samson and John the Baptist were consecrated for life and Paul for a short period.
Nm 6:1-21; Jgs 13:4-5; 1 Mc 3:49; Lk 1:15; Acts 21:20-26.

Oath. A solemn appeal to God to attest the making of a binding promise or the truth of a statement made. Therefore to break or violate it was an offense against God himself.
Gn 21:23,31; 31:53; Ex 20:7; Lv 19:12; Mt 5:33-37; Gal 1:20; Heb 6:16.

Offerings. Sacrifices and oblations of many kinds, both public and private, were a marked feature of Israelite worship. There were drink, cereal, and animal offerings. Libations (drink offerings) were never offered alone. Animal sacrifices were (1) the burnt offering (holocaust); (2) the sin and guilt offerings; and (3) the peace offering (of three types: thank, votive, and freewill).
Lv 1-7. See **Drink, Cereal, Burnt, Sin,** and **Peace Offerings,** all in sec. 4.

Passover (Unleavened Bread). The festival of Passover took place the evening before the fourteenth day of Nisan. Each family was required to offer the sacrifice of a lamb to remember the first such sacrifice: this took place just before the Lord rescued his people from Egypt. The blood of the lamb was sprinkled on the door posts and lintels of the Hebrew houses and seeing this God passed over them and only visited the (Egyptian) houses where no sacrifical blood was to be found. His visit was to slay the firstborn son.

Bread made in haste and without yeast—thus unleavened—was eaten at the Passover meal and all through the following week. This was a reminder of the hurried preparations of the Israelites in leaving Egypt.

All Jews were expected to attend Jerusalem for this festival.
Ex 12; Josh 5:10-12; Mk 14:1-2.

Peace Offering. A sacrifice of thanksgiving to God of which three kinds are distinguished. (1) The thank offering for unexpected and unmerited blessings; (2) the votive offering in payment of a vow; and (3) the freewill offering, an expression of love for God. Any animal normally used in other sacrifices could be used, but the offering of birds was not permitted. Its fat was burnt on the altar, the breast and shoulder went to the priests, and the rest was consumed as a thanksgiving meal by the offerer and his family or friends in the sanctuary.
Lv 3; 7:11f.

Pentecost. See **Weeks, Feast of,** sec. 4.

Pharisee. (Aram, "the separated one"). A Jew who is set apart to obey the Law in wholehearted commitment and rigor. His temptation was to make the Law an end in itself and so lose sight of the more important relationship with God, the giver of the Law.
Mt 23; Lk 13:31; Acts 5:34; 23:6-9.

Phylactery. Two small leather cases, one tied to the left arm and facing the heart, and the other to the forehead of every adult Jew at morning prayer except on the Sabbath. Inside were four essential passages of the Law. The custom derives from Dt 6:8.
Ex 13:1-10; 13:11-13; Dt 6:4-9; 11:13-21; Mt 23:5.

Pilgrimage. A journey to a sacred place for a religious motive. Thus Abraham went to Mount Moriah, and adult Jews were required to travel to the Temple for the statutory festivals.
Gn 22:1-4; Ex 23:14-17; Lk 2:41-42.

Pillar. Apart from their use in architecture, pillars served as memorials of people, covenants, and events as well as marking sacred sites. However, in Canaanite religion the pillars at shrines were venerated, so that the Israelites were commanded to destroy them.
Gn 28:18-22; 31:45-54; 35:20; Ex 23:24; Dt 16:22; Jos 4:1-9; 24:26-27.

Preparation, Day of. The day preceding the Sabbath or the Passover; thus a day of preparation for the feast.
Mt 27:62; Mk 15:42; Lk 23:54; Jn 19:14,31,42.

Presbyter. See **Elder,** sec. 4.

Priest. An authorized minister of God serving in the sanctuary. The Law required a sanctuary and a priesthood, and Aaron and his sons became that priesthood. Their basic duties were to minister in the sanctuary before the Lord, to teach the people the Law, and to inquire the divine will by Urim and Thummim. Their dress included short breeches; a coat fitting closely to the body, woven in one piece; and a cap shaped like a cup. All were made of white linen. Unlike the high priest the ordinary priest was not required to wear an ephod.
Ex 28:1,30; 40:12-15; Nm 16:40; 17:1ff; 18:1-8; Lk 1:5,9.

See **Ephod; Urim and Thummim,** sec. 4.

Prophet. One who announces the word and will of God. The OT prophet did not inherit his office like the priest; he was specially called and empowered by God and then given the divine word. His teaching was always in harmony with that of the Law and was often accredited by signs and by fulfillment of predictions. Some of the prophets wrote down their oracles while the oracles of others were collected by disciples. John the Baptist was the last of the classic OT prophets. The NT prophets only addressed the churches and were individuals with a special endowment of the Holy Spirit. In both OT and NT times, false prophets appeared.
Dt 18:18-19; Is 6; Jer 23:16-32; 1 Cor 12:28; Acts 21:9. See **Prophets, Former and Latter,** sec. 1.

Prophetess. A female prophet. In the OT we read of Miriam, Deborah, and Huldah; in the NT of the four virgin daughters of Philip.
Ex 15:20-21; Nm 12:2; Jgs 4:4; 2 Kgs 22:12-20; Acts 21:9

Proselyte. A Gentile (pagan) converted to Judaism and brought into the Jewish people by circumcision, baptism, and the offering of a sacrifice at the Temple.
Mt 23:15; Acts 2:11; 6:5; 13:43.

Psalms. Hymns of praise, prayer, and lament found in the book of Psalms and used both by Jews and Christians in corporate worship and private devotion.
See **Psalms, Book of,** sec. 1

Purification. The Mosaic law provided for four types of purification from (ritual) uncleanness—due to contact with a corpse or carcass, having suffered a bodily discharge, after childbirth, and after leprosy.
Nm 19; Lv 15; Lv 12:8; Lk 2:21-14; Lv 3,14. See **Clean and unclean,** sec. 4.

Purim, Feast of. Held on the 14 and 15 of the month Adar (February-March) to celebrate the deliverance of the Jewish exiles in Persia from the massacre planned by Haman.
Est 9:20-28; 2 Mc 15:36.

Rabbi (Heb "my master"). A term of respect used by Jews of their instructors in faith and morals.
Mt 23:7-8; Jn 1:38.

Sabbath. The day of rest in order to praise God. Arising from God's own example in his creation and made part of the moral law by its place in the Ten Commandments, the Sabbath was a sacred weekly festival for the Israelites. There were tendencies at one extreme to disregard it and at the other to make it the subject of minute, legalistic rules.
Gn 2:1-3; Ex 20:8-11; Dt 5:12-15; Mk 2:23-28.
See **Sabbath,** sec. 6.

Sacrifices. See **Offerings,** sec. 4.

Sadducees (from Zadok, high priest in king David's reign). A small Jewish party of educated and generally wealthy men, belonging to priestly families. They held to the letter of Scripture and denied both the future resurrection of the dead and the existence of angels. Though they had fundamental disagreements with the Pharisees, they joined them to oppose Jesus, their common enemy.
Mt 22:23-33; Acts 5:17; 23:6-10.

Samaritans. Originally persons living in the old northern kingdom of Israel. Later it was used of inhabitants of central Palestine who were not of pure Israelite stock but who held to the Torah and looked for the coming Messiah.
2 Kgs 17:24f; Ezr 4:1-23; 2 Mc 6:2; Lk 17:11,16; Jn 4:4ff; Acts 8:5-6.

Sanhedrin. The highest assembly or council of the Jews, comprising seventy-one members. In the time of Jesus it met

twice weekly in Jerusalem and had both political and religious functions.
Mt 26:59; Acts 5:21,27; 23:1.

Scribes. Official Jewish interpreters of the Bible, especially the Torah, and sometimes called "lawyers." A man became a scribe at the age of forty after long years of study, and attached to him was a band of disciples. Most scribes belonged to the Pharisees and some were in the Sanhedrin.
1 Mc 7:12; 2 Mc 6:18; Mt 21:15; 23:13f; Acts 4:6; 6:12; 23:9.

Sects (Jewish). Within Judaism in Palestine in the time of Jesus there were several specific groups, who believed that they rightly expressed what Judaism was all about.
See **Essenes, Pharisee, Sadducees, Scribes,** and **Zealot,** sec. 4.

Sin and Guilt Offerings. These may be distinguished in that the former relates chiefly to offences against God directly while the latter relates to offences against human beings. For the sin offering, a bullock or heifer, a male lamb, a dove, or a pigeon could be slaughtered; for the guilt offering, a ram was normally required. No part of either of these offerings was eaten by those who offered them.
Lv 4-7.

Stoics. Disciples of Zeno (336-264 B.C.) who held that within each person is a breath of Universal Reason. Each person must follow this Reason and not be led by passion; wisdom is submission to fate. Paul encountered Stoics in Athens. Acts 17:18.

Synagogue. A Jewish house of prayer, consisting of a hall in which there was a sacred cupboard containing scrolls of the Law and Prophets. The leader was a local layman, chosen by the local men. Used for day-school and on the Sabbath for

worship. Paul began his missionary work in them.
Lk 4:16ff; Acts 17:10-12.

Tabernacles, Feast of. See **Booths, Feast of,** sec. 4.

Tammuz. A deity of the Babylonians, who gave his name to the fourth month of the Semitic ritual year.
Ez 6:14.

Temple. Although reference is made to temples of various deities, e.g., to Dagon, the interest of Scripture is in the three successive Temples of Jerusalem. These replaced the Tent of Meeting or Tabernacle as the central shrine where God met with his people. (1) *Solomon's Temple.* Taking seven and a half years to build, this was a magnificent building; it was plundered and burned by the Babylonians in 586 B.C. (2) *Zerubbabel's Temple.* On a smaller scale than Solomon's, this was completed by the returning exiles from Babylon in 515 B.C. (3) *Herod's Temple.* On a much larger scale than that of Zerubbabel and even greater than that of Solomon, this was begun in 19 B.C. and not completed until A.D. 64. At its center was the holy of holies surrounded by the court of priests and court of men, with the women's court nearby, and then on the outer part the court of the Gentiles. This was the Temple Jesus knew; it was destroyed by the Romans in A.D. 70.
2 Sm 7; 1 Kgs 5:3-5; 8:17; 2 Kgs 25:8-17; 1 Chr 22; 28:11ff; Ezr 4-6; 1 Mc 4:36ff; Mt 21:12ff. See **Tent of Meeting,** sec. 4.

Tent of Meeting (Tabernacle, Tent of Witness). Erected on the first day of the second year after the departure of the Israelites from Egypt. It was made of materials available in the wilderness: acacia wood, hair and skins from the flocks, gold and jewels from the people. Here God met with his covenant people. Within the Tent were the Ark, the table of showbread, the lampstand, altars, and a laver. A cloud rested

on it by day and a pillar of fire by night. When the Israelites moved camp, the Levites dismantled it and erected it at the new site. In Canaan it was first kept at Gilgal and later at Shiloh; then the Temple was built and the Tent of Meeting became redundant.
Ex 25-40; Jos 18:1; Heb 9:11-14,23-27.

Thank Offering. See **Peace Offering,** sec. 4.

Thummim. See **Urim and Thummim,** sec. 4.

Tithe. A tenth part devoted to God. According to the Law of Moses the tithe included the yearly grain, wine, and oil. Together with the firstlings of the flock and herd, it was given to the Levites and Priests.
Dt 14:22f; 2 Chr 31:5; Neh 10:38; Tb 1:7; Mal 3:10.

Trumpets (later **New Year**). On the first day of the seventh month, trumpets sounded for a special celebration. It was a festival day, a day for rest and worship. This was because it heralded the arrival of the seventh month, the holiest of all months. After the Exile it was known as the New Year Festival because the seventh month is the beginning of the civil (not religious) year.
Num 10:10; 28:9; 29:1-2; Lv 23:24.

Unleavened Bread, Feast of. See **Passover,** sec. 4.

Urim and Thummim (literally, "lights" and "perfections, truths"). Small objects belonging to the ephod of the high priest, which were placed in his breastpiece of judgment. Thus they were next to his heart when he went in before the Lord in the inner sanctuary. On his exit, they were probably thrown like dice and by their fall revealed the divine will for the nation (not individuals). They seem not to have been used after David's time.
Ex 28:30; Lv 8:8; Nm 27:21; Dt 33:8; 1 Sm 14:41; 28:6; Ezr 2:63; Neh 7:65.

Vestments of the Priests. The high priest's liturgical dress was a breastpiece, an ephod, a robe, a brocaded tunic, a miter, and a sash. Its colors were gold, violet, purple, and scarlet, in yarn and linen. Both the ephod and breastpiece were adorned wih fine stones.

The ordinary priest was much less magnificently dressed, being essentially clothed in white linen.
Ex 28-29. See **Ephod** and **High Priest,** sec. 4.

Votive offering. See **Peace Offering** and **Vow,** sec. 4.

Vow. A voluntary obligation to God in the belief that he will bestow his favor. The Law of Moses regulated rather than prescribed vows, e.g., the vow of devotion by which a person or possessions were given to God's sanctuary, and the vow of abstinence. Once made, a vow was normally compulsory.
Gn 28:18-22; Lv 27:1-34; Acts 18:18.

Wave Offering. In connection with certain sacrifices and offerings in the Temple, a part of the animal or the crop was physically waved before the Lord. That which had been waved then went to the priests.
Ex 29:24-27; Lv 7:30; 10:14-15; 14:21-24; 23:11-20; Nm 6:20; 8:11-21.

Weeks, Feast of. So called because it was held seven weeks (fifty days, hence Pentecost) after the offering of the sheaf of the first-ripe barley; it was the first of the two agricultural festivals and was concerned with the harvest of grain. It was treated as a Sabbath, and special offerings were made in the Temple. At the Pentecost immediately following the Resurrection of Jesus, the Holy Spirit descended upon the waiting disciples.
Lv 23:9-22; Nm 28:26-31; Dt 16:11-12; Acts 2:1-4.

Zealot. A member of a Jewish patriotic, revolutionary party, begun by Judas the Galilean in the time of Quirinius. Simon the apostle had belonged to this group.
Mt 10:4; Mk 3:18; Lk 6:15; Acts 1:13.

FIVE

Culture and Customs

Armor and Weapons. The Bible mentions such items as shields, helmets, and coats of mail with greaves (bronze armor over the shins) as examples of soldiers' defensive armor. Among the wide range of weapons available in biblical times, Scripture specifically mentions swords, spears, javelins, bows and arrows, slings, and battle-axes.
Jos 10:11; 11:11; Jgs 5:8; 1 Sm 17:5-7; 17:38; 22:6; 31:9-10; 1 Kgs 22:34f; 1 Chr 5:8; 12:2; 1 Mc 6:35; Jer 51:20; Is 59:17; Eph 6:13-17.

Arts and Crafts. From archaeological evidence and the text of Scripture, we know that the following are some of the trades or crafts which flourished from OT into NT times: pottery, stonemasonry, carpentry, metalwork (copper, iron, gold, silver), tanning and leatherwork, dyeing, fulling (with cleansing and bleaching).
Jer 18:3-4; Mt 13:55; Mk 6:3; 1 Kgs 6:7; 7:9; 1 Sm 13:19-22; Prv 17:3; 27:21; Acts 9:43; 12:6,32; Ex 26:1,31; 36:8; Lv 14:4; 2 Kgs 18:17; Is 7:3; 36:2.

Boats. See **Ships and Boats,** sec. 5.

Burial. Corpses, partially or wholly embalmed, were usually buried in caverns, natural or man-made, outside the town. Each family normally had its own tomb. Before and after burial, vocal and demonstrative mourning was common.
Gn 50:13; Dt 21:22-23; 34:5-8; 2 Kgs 23:6; Wis 22:12; 38:16-18; Mk 5:38; Mt 9:23; Lk 18:13; 23:48; Acts 9:39.

Calendar. Though an agricultural people, the Israelites used a lunar calendar, whose year began in our March of April. The twelve months were Nisan, Iyyar, Sivan, Tammuz, Ab, Elul, Tishri, Marchevan, Chislev, Tebeth, Shebat, and Adar. By NT times there were differences amongst Pharisees, Sadducees, and sectarian groups as to when the year began, i.e., the fixing of Lv 23:15.
Est 3:7; Neh 2:1; Est 8:9; Neh 6:15; 1:1; Est 2:16; Zc 1:7.

Chariot. The Israelites in Egypt were familiar with chariots and, on leaving the country, were pursued by them. On entering Canaan they found chariots used by the rulers of the low-lying city-states; but only in the reign of Solomon did chariots become a part of the Israelite army. He established chariot cities at Hazor, Magiddo, Gezer, and Jerusalem. The Israelite chariot had two horses and three men (driver, defender, and fighter).
Gn 41:43; 46:29; 50:9; Jos 17:16; Jgs 1:19; 1 Sam 13:5; 1 Kgs 9:15-19; 10:16-29; Acts 8:28.

Cities of Refuge. Six levitical cities were available for shelter for those who had accidentally committed manslaughter.
Nm 35:9-14; Ex 21:13

City. Israelites were aware of large cities—e.g., Pithom and Raamses in Egypt, Damascus in Syria, and the massive Nineveh and Babylon. In settling in Canaan they came across many small, fortified cities, many of which they took over, Jerusalem being the most important. Near the (usually) large gate, business was transacted and cases of law adjudicated. Jerusalem, known as the city of God, came to symbolize God's dwelling place in heaven where the righteous ever worship their Lord.
Dt 3:5; Est 9:19; 1 Kgs 16:24; Mt 5:14; 2 Sm 18:33; Ru 4:1-11; 1 Kgs 22:10; Neh 8:1; Rv 21-22.

Cosmetics. See **Perfume,** sec. 5.

Crime and Punishment. Since God is always seen as the supreme Judge, the Bible contains a deeply religious interpretation of law, crime, transgression, and punishment. In some ways the provisions of the Law of Moses is similar to other near Eastern law codes, e.g., on the matter of blood revenge (Ex 21:23-25). However, what is unique in the Mosaic code is that laws in the direct style (e.g., "you shall not kill") are presented as direct commands of God and that the whole corpus of laws of both direct and indirect type is seen as being inspired by God. In fact, law is seen as setting forth what God requires, and thus deliberate breaking of it is an offense not only against a person wronged but also against the Lawgiver himself. Violation of the religious duties of the covenant (e.g., murder, idolatry, sorcery, and neglect of feasts), immorality and unchastity (e.g., bestiality, sodomy, and incest), insubordination and refusal to submit to lawful authority (e.g., of parent or priest), and crimes against the person (e.g., injury, stealing, and false witness) were punished by death (via stoning), whipping, retaliation, compensation and fine, forfeiture of rights, or loss of a hand. Ex 21-22; Dt 13; 22; Lv 20; 24; Nm 25.

Crucifixion. Jews did not practice this but sometimes they hung dead bodies from a tree as a warning. In the Roman Empire, slaves, provincials, and criminals (and only rarely Roman citizens) were crucified. As well as the familiar cross shape, the type of cross on which Jesus died, crosses in an **X** or **T** shape were also used. Before crucifixion the victim was scourged and then made to carry part of his cross.
Dt 21:22-23; Gal 3:13; Mt 27:37.

Disease. See **Health and Disease,** sec. 5.

Education. In biblical times parents had the duty of educating their children. Parents taught their children morality, religion, reading, and arithmetic; the father taught

his trade to his son and the mother passed on domestic skills to her daughter. With the arrival of the synagogue in the latter part of the OT period, instruction in the Bible and morality was available for all age-groups. For those who desired to become rabbis there was instruction at the feet of (seated) distinguished rabbis. Certain books of the OT have the character of educational texts—Proverbs, Wisdom, Sirach.
Dt 4:9; Acts 22:3; Eph 6:1,4.

Family. In early Israelite history the family meant the clan or tribe, united by common descent and blood. Within the clan were the smaller units of man, wife, and children. By the time of king Solomon, these smaller units were occupying small houses. It was, however, from the wider clan that the parents chose a daughter to be a wife for their son, who left her own small family to join his. Parents wanted many children, especially males; the eldest son inherited a double portion and became head of the family.

In Roman society the household consisted not only of the master, his wife, children, and slaves but also of resident friends and employees. Often churches began within such households.
Lv 18:6-18; Jos 7:16-18; Ps 127:3-5; Acts 16:15,31-34.

Food. In the land of Israel, the three basic commodities were grain (barley, wheat), wine (from the vine), and olive oil. Apart from grapes, fruit included figs and pomegranates; vegetables included lentils and beans. Animal products were milk (butter, cheese) and certain types of meat (ox, sheep, goat); certain insects (e.g., locusts) were eaten, as also was wild honey.
Dt 7;13; Neh 5:11; 2 Sm 17:28; 3:11; Dt 8:8; Hos 1:8; 1 Kgs 4:7-28. See **Wine and Strong Drink,** sec. 5.

Health and Disease. The Law of Moses contains (for its time) a remarkable sanitary code and provision for public health. In the Bible God is seen as the one who heals diseases, naturally or supernaturally, and in certain cases as the one who sends diseases as punishment to sinners. The use of such remedies as were known was not held to conflict with the belief in God as Healer. Miraculous healing was rare in the OT (except in the ministries of Elijah and Elisha), but it is a distinctive feature of the ministry of Jesus and his apostles.

The most common diseases recorded in the Bible were (in non-technical terms): female barrenness; blindness; boils; skin disorders; consumption; deafness; dropsy; dumbness; dysentery; epilepsy; fever; inflammation; itching (eczema); leprosy; mental disorder; paralysis; plague; scab or spots; and the results of demon possession.
Lv 12; 15; Ps 103:3; Ex 9:8ff; 1 Sm 1:10ff; Dt 28:28-29; Lv 13:18ff; 26:16; 19:14; 2 Chr 21:15 19; Mt 17:15; Dt 28:22; Lv 13-14.

Jewelry and Precious Stones. The fullest list of precious stones in the OT is in the description of the breastpiece of the high priest, and in the NT it is in the description of the decoration of the New Jerusalem. In Biblical times many different precious and semiprecious stones were used in jewelry.
Ex 28:17-20; 39:10-13; Rv 21:19f; Is 3:18-21; 2 Chr 20:25.

King and Kingship. Early Israel had no king. It was the crisis caused by the Philistines in Palestine that caused the tribes of Israel to call for a king and a settled army. The first king, Saul, was a military chieftain. As an institution, kingship developed rapidly under David and Solomon. They based their administration on the system in use in Egypt. However, because the Law of Moses existed before monarchy, the kings of Israel were never law-makers, only judges. After the division of the kingdom, there were separate kings in the North (Israel) and South (Judah) until the collapse of both kingdoms. On the return from Exile in Babylon, the Jews never had a true king again. Herod and his sons merely

ruled by the permission of Rome. The longing for a righteous king, ruling in justice, led to the hope of a Messiah, fulfilled in Jesus.
1 Sm 8:4-22; 1 Kgs 3:28; 9:4-5; Jn 18:36.

Money. Coins were introduced into the ancient Near East in the seventh century B.C. Before then (as after) transactions were by barter, which could make use of gold or silver or copper. In their exile in Babylon the Jews first met coinage, that of Darius I of Persia.

In NT times money from three different sources was circulating in Palestine: Rome, Antioch (Greek), and Jerusalem. Hence the need for moneychangers at the Temple in Jerusalem. Money was coined in gold, silver, and copper. The only Jewish coin mentioned in the NT is the widow's mite (the bronze *lepton*) but the primary unit was the silver *shekel.* The basic Greek coin was the silver *drachma* and the basic Roman coin the silver *denarius.*
Ez 2:69; 8:27; Mt 10:9; Mk 12:42; Lk 15:8; Mt 18:28.

Music. Music played an important part in the life of the people of Israel—in joy and sadness, in community worship and celebration. There were choirs in the Temple and a variety of instruments were used in worship and social occasions. Stringed instruments included the harp, ten-stringed lyre, and the ordinary lyre; wind instruments included different types of horn, trumpet, and pipe; and percussion instruments included the cymbal, bells, and sistrum.
Ex 15:20; 28:33-34; Jos 6:4; 1 Sm 10:5; 1 Chr 15:16-24; Ps 81:2.

Name. Personal names are often significant in the Bible. God's name of *Yahweh* and the name *Jesus* for the eternal Son incarnate are always significant. While some children received a name merely because the parents liked it, a name (by human intention or divine providence) came to be signifi-

cant in terms of circumstance (e.g., Moses and Samuel), status (woman, Jehoiakim), occasion (Cain), transformation (Peter), prediction (Isaiah's two sons), admonition (James and John "Boanerges"), or a prayer (Nabal). Jesus' name reflects status, is predictive, and is also a name of fulfilment.
Ex 3:14; 2:10; 1 Sm 1:20; Gn 2:23; 2 Kgs 23:34; Gn 4:1; Jn 1:42; Is 7:3; 8:1-4,18; Mk 3:17; 1 Sm 25:25; Mt 1:23.

Number. Some numbers are sometimes used to convey a meaning other than their numerical value. Thus seven (in Creation God rested on the seventh day) points to completion and fullness while forty (Jesus was in the wilderness forty days and on earth forty days after his resurrection) is a round number. Since there are ten fingers, and ten is the basis of the decimal system, ten is also a number of fullness and completion. So also is twelve (from the Sumerian sexagesimal system), thus twelve tribes and apostles.
Gn 2:2; Mt 4:2; Mk 10:1-4; Acts 1:3.

Oil. The produce of the olive fruit was extremely important. It was used as a medicine, fuel for lamps, and for cooking; also for anointing the body after a bath, as a chrism at the consecration of priests and kings, and as a part of the daily offering in the Temple.
1 Kgs 17:12-16; Ps 23:5; Is 1:6; 42:3; Ex 29:2; 22:9; Dt 12:17; Ru 3:3.

Perfume. The fragrance of spices (e.g., aloes, cassia, cinnamon, myrrh, frankincense, spikenard) was released by such methods as being tied to a small bag, reduced to powder to burn as incense, mixed with oil to make ointment, and the essence extracted to make scent. All palaces had perfumeries where the process was akin to cooking; petals of flowers were continually dropped into hot oil. Perfume was applied to the body, to garments, and to furniture; it was also used in the Temple.

Ex 30:22-25; 1 Sm 8:13; Prv 7:17; Sg 1:3,13; 36; 4:11; Sir 24:15.

Sackcloth. A coarse cloth, normally black in color and made from goats' hair. Worn by shepherds as normal dress and put on specially by prophets and ordinary people as a sign of penitence or mourning.
Gn 37:34; Jb 16:15; 1 Mc 2:14; Is 20:2; Rv 11:3.

Ships and Boats. The small boats of the Sea of Galilee, with sail and oars, were used both for fishing and transportation. On the Mediterranean, there were larger ships (usually from 70 to 300 tons) also having sails and oars. The largest were the grain ships sailing from Egypt to Italy. Paul traveled on a ship which had 276 passengers and crew. Ships were normally dismasted and laid up to avoid the winter storms (November-February).

Solomon, in alliance with the Phoenicians, built a merchant fleet based in the Gulf of Aqaba, and traded with Arabia.
1 Kgs 9:26-28; 1 Mc 15:3-4; Mk 1:19; Acts 27.

Slavery. Throughout the period covered by the OT and NT, slavery was common. A person became a slave for one of various reasons: by capture in war, by purchase, by birth (from a slave), as restitution, by having defaulted on debts, through selling oneself, and by abduction. In the Law of Moses, the laws governing slavery were generally more humane than in other contemporary law codes. In the NT it is only household slavery concerning which the apostles give instruction, though in Jesus' parables there is reference to slaves working on farms.
Gn 15:3; 37:27-28; 45:4; Ex 22:3; Lv 25:39-43; 25:44-55; Mt 21:34; Col 3:22; 1 Tm 6:1-3.

Trade. Palestine was geographically well placed for trade by land, standing at the junction of Egypt, Arabia, and Asia

Minor. Goods carried by camel caravan for Israel included: (1) exports: olive oil, cereals, fruit, honey, nuts, aromatic gum, myrrh, wool, and woven garments; (2) imports: tin, lead, silver, copper, timber, linen, spices, precious stones, gold, and silver. In OT times the great period of trade was in the time of the kings. In NT times imports also included cotton and silk from the East, wines, glass bowls, apples, cheese, and slaves. Sea trade was never as important to Israel as that by land.
1 Kgs 5; 10; 22:48-49; Ez 27; Mt 25:14.

Travel. Ordinary people either walked or sat on an ass. Caravans were convoys of camels, asses, and people involved in trade. Horses were usually kept for pulling chariots in war. On farms, carts were pulled by asses or oxen. People in OT times traveled for trade, to attend religious festivals, or, in emergencies, in migration due to famine or war. With the arrival of the Roman Empire, travel was made easier by land (on the network of paved roads) and sea. The expansion of Christianity owed much to this facility.
Gn 46:5; Nm 20:17; 1 Kgs 9:26-28; Mk 4:35-39; Acts 27.

See **Ships and Boats** and **Trade,** sec. 5.

Weights and measures. Ancient weights were stones shaped as birds or animals and with flat bases. A talent (30 kg), mina (500 gm), shekel (10 gm) pim (7 gm), beka (5 gm), and gerah (0.5 gm) were these of OT and NT times. Linear measurement was based on familiar units: a finger (1.85 cm), palm (7.40 cm), span (22.25 cm), cubit (44.5 cm), and reed (2.67 m). In NT times there is also the fathom (2.10 m), stade (185 m) and mile (1478.8 m). Capacity was measured by the homer (220 liters), ephah (22 liters), hin (3.6 liters) and log (0.3 liters).
Ex 30:13; Lv 19:36; 1 Kgs 10:14; 17; Ezek 40:5; Mt 6:27; Lk 24:13; See **Money,** sec. 5.

Wine and Strong Drink. The juice of the grape was normally red and plentiful in Palestine. It was used as fresh juice; as must (sweet wine) straight from the winepress; as wine after fermentation; and as vinegar. A light wine, mixed with water, was part of the staple diet. It could also act as a medicine. There are warnings in the OT and NT about drinking to excess.

"Strong drink" was made from the juice of other fruit (e.g., dates), from honey, and from barley.
Is 63:2; Jer 48:11-12; Prov 31:6; Mt 26:9; Lk 1:15.

Writing. From the second millennium B.C. when alphabets were developed, virtually any smooth surface was used for writing: stone, boards of wood or ivory, clay tablets, papyrus, leather, parchment, and potsherds. The usual form of a book in biblical times was a roll or scroll of papyrus, leather, or parchment. From the second century A.D. the roll was replaced by the codex, a collection of sheets similar to a modern book.
Jb 19:24; Hab 2:2; Ez 4:1; 2 Jn 12; Dt 6:9; 11:20. See **Aramaic, Greek,** and **Hebrew,** sec. 1.

SIX

Doctrine

Angels(messengers). Spiritual beings who exist to serve God and to praise the Lord. Higher in status than humans, they are lower in status than the exalted Jesus. Among them there are different ranks or orders, including angels and archangels. Some rebelled against God's sovereignty; their leader is known as Satan (the devil), and they became fallen or disobedient angels. The vast majority, however, have remained as free obedient beings, and it was they who welcomed the birth of Jesus and will come with him at his Second Coming. In the OT, the "angel of the Lord" is in fact God himself speaking. Two angels are specifically named in the OT, Gabriel and Raphael. Gabriel appeared again to announce the Incarnation. Michael, the "prince of Israel" is also often referred to as an angel.
Heb 1:14; Mt 22:30; Jb 1:6; 38:7; Jude 9; 2 Kgs 6:17; Ps 34:17; Dan 8:16; 9:21; Gn 16:17; 21:17-19; Ex 32:34; 33:14; Mt 1:20,24.

Apostle (emissary). Used of Jesus, its general meaning is to describe those sent by him, empowered by his Spirit to proclaim his message. The twelve chosen by Jesus are called apostles: they were Peter, Andrew, James, John, Philip, Bartholomew, Matthew, Thomas, James, Thaddeus (or Jude), Simon, and Judas Iscariot. When Judas Iscariot defected, he was replaced by Matthias, but when James was martyred he was not replaced. Peter is the leader of this group, and they have a unique place in the origin and content of Christianity and the church.

Others, such as Barnabas, were called apostles because they were involved in evangelism, teaching, founding churches, and assisting the apostles.

Finally, Saul of Tarsus was specially called to be the "apostle to the Gentiles."
Heb 3:1; Mt 10:2-4; Lk 6:14-16; Acts 1:13; Acts 13:3; 14:4; Eph 2:20; Acts 9:15; 22:21; Gal 1:15f; Rom 1:5; 11:13.

Ascension. After his resurrection, Jesus regularly appeared in his immortal body to his disciples for forty days. Then he made his final departure dramatically into a cloud (symbol of the Lord's presence). This special and final departure is usually called "the Ascension," even though Jesus actually was exalted into heaven on Easter day and thus the resurrection appearances were from heaven. By his Ascension and exaltation, Jesus was designated the Messiah, the Lord and Head of the church as he "sat at the right hand" of God, from there sending the Holy Spirit to his people.
Lk 4:50-53; Acts 1:3-11; Phil 2:5-11.

Atonement. See **Blood** and **Reconciliation,** sec. 6.

Authority. God possesses ultimate authority since, as the Creator and Judge, he alone has the power and right to control creatures and creation. As universal King, he alone has rightful power and thus all power to act within the universe is delegated by him; further, submission to authority is the way of serving God. In terms of Israel, he exercised his Lordship within the covenant through the authority given to the prophets, priests, and kings to speak and act according to his revealed will in the Law.

Jesus possessed authority (*exousia*) to speak and act in God's name since he was the Messiah and had been sent by God. In turn, the power to act as apostles and proclaim the

gospel was the authority possessed by Jesus as Messiah and delegated to them. The authority given by apostles to elders and bishops within local churches was also the delegated authority of Jesus, the Messiah.
Ps 29:10; 93:1; Dn 4:32-37; Mt 8:9; 28:18-19; Acts 2:36; Jn 17:18; 20:21; 1 Pt 5:1f; Rom 13:1-6; 1 Pt 3:1-6.

Baptism, Christian. According to Christ's command, all converts to Christianity were baptized in water and promised baptism in the Holy Spirit. Seen as much more than being plunged into water, the event was interpreted as a dying and rising with Christ, a new birth, a seal, a heavenly illumination, a new circumcision, a bath of regeneration, and a new creation in Christ.
Acts 2:41; 8:12,16,36,38; Rom 6:3-5; Col 2:12; 1 Pt 3:18-21, Jn 3:5; 2 Cor 1:22; Eph 1:13; 4:30; 5:8-14; Heb 6:4; Col 2:11; Ti 3:5; 2 Cor 5:17. See **Baptism,** sec. 4.

Bishop. See **Episcope,** sec. 6.

Blood. The blood of animals was seen as being the life, created by God. However, in terms of sacrificial offerings according to the Law of Moses, the blood usually referred to the violent death of the victim. Atonement for sin and pollution was gained by the sacrificial offering involving the death of the victim and the pouring out of blood.

In the NT, the "blood of Christ" is an OT way of speaking of the sacrificial, atoning death of Jesus by which reconciliation between God and his creation was achieved. Further, the wine at the Last Supper, the night before Jesus' crucifixion, points to the shed blood of Jesus, by which a new covenant was sealed.
Lv 4; 17:11; Nm 35:33; Ex 29:33; Lv 10; 17; Rom 5:9-10; Col 1:20; 1 Jn 5:6; Mt 26:27f.

Christ. See **Messiah,** sec. 6.

Church. The community of the baptized, those who have

responded to the call of God in the gospel concerning Jesus Christ. Thus it is the church of God, and its head, life-giver, and dispenser of spiritual gifts is Jesus. The Greek word is *ekklesia,* the word used in the Septuagint of the assembly of Israel called to meet with God. Normally in the NT, *ekklesia* is a local church—in Jerusalem or Antioch, for example—with its own officers (elders and deacons). However, *ekklesia* also is used of the total assembly of the baptized who exist simultaneously in various churches (and as martyrs in heaven). The ministry of apostles was to the scattered churches, and Jesus called Peter a rock of the whole church. A variety of images is used in the NT to convey the nature and characteristics of the church, e.g., body, body of Christ, temple of the spirit, household of faith.
Mt 16:16; 18:17; Acts 8:1; Rom 16:4; 1 Cor 1:2; Eph 1:15-22; Col 1:18f; Rv 1:4.

Confession. Both a public commitment to God as Redeemer and King and an acknowledgement of guilt before him for sin. Both aspects are found in the OT and NT. However, in the NT, confession of Jesus—as Messiah, Son of God and exalted Lord—is central. Later Creeds and Confessions of Faith are to be traced to these simple apostolic statements. Confession of sin is closely related to repentance and faith. Further, the person who confesses Jesus as Lord in this world will be acknowledged by Jesus at his Second Coming.
Neh 9:3; Ps 32:5; 46:11; 68:35; Rom 10:9; 14:11-12; Mt 10:32-33.

Conversion. Turning away from sin and back to God in repentance and faith. In the OT, Israel as a people is repeatedly called by the prophets to turn back in repentance and faith to its covenant God, the Lord. Only a few individual conversions are described. The conversion of a pagan city, Nineveh, is presented.

John the Baptist called the Jewish people to repentance and preparation for the coming kingdom of God. As the

Messiah, whom John promised would come, Jesus proclaimed the need for repentance and faith by each and every Jew in the face of the arriving kingdom. After his Ascension, and following the gift of the Spirit, the early church called upon Jew and Gentile to repent of sin and turn in faith to the Lord Jesus. Baptism was the sign of conversion.
Dt 4:29f; 30:2,10; Is 6:9f; Ps 51:13; 2 Kgs 5; 23:25; Jon 3:7-10; Mt 3:2; 4:17; 11:20-24; Lk 24:47; Acts 3:19; 11:21; 26:20.

Covenants. Within the culture of the ancient near East, the idea of an alliance or covenant between the deity and the king (or people) was common. Thus the Lord used this form of relationship for his adoption of individuals, families, and peoples as his servants and children. We read of covenants between God and Noah; God and Abraham; God and the tribes of Israel at Mount Sinai; God and King David; and God and Jesus (as the substitute and representative man). The latter, called the new covenant, is in certain ways a republication of the Abrahamic covenant of grace and fulfilment of the Sinai and Davidic covenants.
Gn 6:18; 9:8-17; 15; 17; Ex 24; 2 Sm 7; Mk 14:22-25; 1 Cor 11:23-25.

Creation. "Through faith we perceive that the worlds were created by the word of God, and that what is visible came into being through the invisible" (Heb 11:3). The fact that God is the creator, upholder, and preserver of the universe is a revealed truth, which God invites us to accept. He made the universe out of nothing; he uttered his creative and life-giving word and the universe was made and is maintained.

Genesis 1:1-2:4, depicting the seven days of creation, is written by someone imagining he was present in the style of an eyewitness account. In other parts of the OT there are echoes of various pagan myths of creation, e.g., of the Lord victorious in combat with Leviathan, but the consistent message is that God created the world through his Word

(the Son). Within the created order, mankind is to be God's steward. At the end of time, the present created world will be renewed in order to become part of the "new heavens and earth" of the new order of the kingdom of God.
Jn 1:3; Acts 17:25; Col 1:16; Rev 4:11; Is 27:1f; Rev 21. See **Genesis,** sec. 1.

Disciple. Those who sat at the feet of the great prophets and teachers of Israel were called "servants." Only in the late OT period did the word "disciple" come into use to describe the servants of the experts in the Law (rabbi) from whom they learned. In the NT, the word is only found in the Gospels and Acts. Both John the Baptist and Jesus, even though they were not "official" teachers of Judaism, had their disciples. Jesus was popularly known as a rabbi and thus those who responded to his message, those who traveled around the country with him, and those whom he particularly chose as the inner circle of his associates were all called disciples. To be a disciple meant personal allegiance to Jesus and giving him exclusive loyalty as the Messiah. In the early church, those who were baptized were known as disciples of Jesus. In other parts of the NT (Epistles), disciples are called "saints," "believers," and "brethren."
1 Chr 25:8; Mk 2:18; Jn 1:35; Mk 9:5; Mt 5:1; Mk 6:45; 3:14; Acts 6:1f.

Election. God's act of choosing people in order that they may reflect his character and do his will. The faith of the people of Israel was based on the conviction that God had chosen them and had made a covenant with Abraham and Moses. By these holy alliances they were his people. Further, specific individuals (e.g., Moses, Aaron, kings, and prophets) were chosen by God to help the whole people live as the elect of God. Election brought wonderful blessings, but failure to keep the covenant meant forfeiture of those blessings.

Election in the NT is centered on Jesus Christ who is the

elect One of the Father; further, those who are united to him in God's grace by the Spirit and baptism are also the elect. At the final judgment, those who are judged righteous are the elect. Election proceeds from God's free and gracious love; and it places responsibility upon those elected that they live worthy of their calling.
Gn 11:31-12:7; Ex 24; Dt 6:21-23; 7:6; 28:1-14; Lev 20;26; Ps 106:23; 105:26; Is 42:1; 49:1,5; Lk 9:35; 1 Pt 2:9; Eph 1; Rom 11:5.

Episcope. The presiding over and oversight of a local church. In NT times this duty was exercised by those called deacons, presbyters (elders), and bishops (*episcopoi*). Only gradually did the threefold ministry of bishop, priest, and deacon develop so that episcope was the primary responsibility of the bishop. In fact, the terms bishop and presbyter were used of one and the same person to denote his office and his function. Ultimately all episcope belongs to Christ, the good shepherd.
Acts 20:17; 20:28; Tit 1:5,7; 1 Tm 3:1-12; 1 Pt 2:25; 5:4.

Eschatology (study of the end). That which relates to the last and final events in this present age, together with the nature and character of the new age to follow this age. The prophets of Israel speak of universal judgment and the establishment of God's kingdom; Jesus promised that he would return with the holy angels as Judge and to inaugurate the new age; likewise the apostles speak of his return, the judgment, and the new age.

There is, however, a sense in which by the death and resurrection of Jesus and through the sending of the Holy Spirit the new age has (in principle) already arrived and the old age has (effectively) been judged.
Zc 14:9; Is 65:17; 66:22; Mt 19:28; Mk 13; 1 Thes 4:4-17; 1 Cor 15:23; 10:11; Jude 18; Acts 2:17; Heb 1:2.

Ethics. Biblical moral teaching is essentially God-centered

in that it proceeds from the character and will of God, who is holy and good. Thus, "Be holy for I am holy" (Lv 19:2); "Be made perfect as your heavenly Father is perfect" (Mt 5:48); and "God is love . . . therefore love" (1 Jn 4). Religion and ethics are inseparable. In the OT the ethics are the basic moral principles contained in the covenantal duties which the Israelites owe to the God who elected them; they relate both to social justice and personal morality. The Ten Commandments are prefaced by God's declaration that he is the redeemer of Israel. The ethics of Jesus are those of the kingly reign of God and are the fulfilment of the ethics of the OT. He is the exemplar of love.
Ex 20; Mk 12:28f; Lk 10:29; 1 Jn 4:7-12.

Expiation and Propitiation. Sin is a barrier between human beings and God: it is also an offense to him. Propitiation is an act that appeases or removes the wrath of God against sin; it is a word which presupposes a personal relationship between sinners and God, their judge and redeemer. Expiation is an act of blotting out, cleansing, or casting away of sin. In referring to the sacrificial, atoning death of Jesus, we may think of it as a propitiation, or an expiation, or both a propitiation and expiation.
Rom 3:25; 1 Jn 2:2; 4:10. See **Reconciliation,** sec. 6.

Faith. In the OT, the word "faith" is rare, but the concept is conveyed by the use of such verbs as "believe," "trust," and "hope." Abraham exemplifies faith for he believed and obeyed God unreservedly. The basis of the covenant of Sinai from the Israelite side was the accepting and believing God in his self-revelation in the Law and saving acts. The prophets persistently called the people to believe, to trust, and to obey their God.

In the NT, faith is obviously an important concept and the word is common. Jesus called for faith in God as the Father and in himself as the Messiah. The apostles called for faith in, and commitment to, Jesus as God's divinely appointed

Messiah and Lord. In particular, St. Paul emphasized faith centered on Christ and active in love as the primary response of sinners to the gospel of God. St. James emphasized that merely believing the facts of the gospel was not enough; true faith results in acts of love. True faith is faithful to God for it means both believing or trusting and obeying.
Dt 32:20; Hab 2:4; Gn 12:1-2; 15:1-6; Rom 4:18-22; Mk 11:22; Mt 18:6; Jn 14:1; Lk 11:28; Gal 5:25; 6:8; Jas 2:17-26.

Fall, The. A way of expressing the fact that the human race is not what God intended it to be; it has fallen from a position of perfect spiritual union with himself to that of fear of, or enmity towards, him, and thus is in need of salvation. In fact, the reality of human sinfulness and need for communion with God is everywhere assumed in the OT and NT, and against this background the message of grace, mercy, and salvation is provided. The Hebrew account of the Fall, the first act of disobedience of human beings against God and thus the loss of intimate fellowship, is found in Genesis 3.
Sir 25:24; Wis 2:22-25; Rom 5:12-14; 1 Cor 15:21; 1 Tim 2:13-14.

Forgiveness. Because God is gracious, he forgives penitent and believing people. That is, he removes their guilt as far as the east is from the west; he blots it out and he remembers it no more. Yet sin merits punishment and thus atonement was provided in the OT by sacrifices according to the Law of Moses; in the NT forgiveness is for Christ's sake, for his atoning sacrifice. The act of forgiveness by God is thus costly and those who are forgiven are to imitate God by forgiving others. Forgiveness is thus a central part of the message of the gospel of God for sinners.
Ps 51:1,9; 103:12; 130:4; Ex 34:6f; Is 38:17; 43:25; Jer 31:34; Ne 9:17; Mk 2:10; Mt 26:28; Acts 5:31; Eph 1:7; Lk 6:37; Col 3:13.

Glory. Shorthand for the self-disclosure by God of his holy

being and character. In the OT this revelation was usually in the context of specific physical phenomena, e.g., the luminous cloud which led the Israelites in the wilderness in the days of Moses and which later rested upon the Temple. In the NT, God's glory is reflected in Jesus Christ, especially in such events as his transfiguration, death, resurrection, and Ascension, and especially at his second coming.
Ex 16:7,10; 24:15-18; 40:34-35; Lv 9:6,23; Is 6:1-4; 40:4-5; Mk 9:2-8; Jn 12:23-28; Lk 24:26; Mk 8:38; 13:26; 2 Cor 4:3-6.

God. As the record of the divine self-revelation to mankind, the Bible takes God's existence for granted. He is the self-existent Creator: while everyone and everything is dependent upon him, he is dependent on nothing. He is all-powerful and all-knowing. In relation to the universe he is both transcendent (totally above and detached) and immanent (wholly present as the source of life). Yet he is a personal God who relates to human beings in and through personal relationships; in these he reveals himself as perfectly wise, holy, and compassionate. Although human beings have free will and sometimes abuse its privileges, God's sovereign will and purpose for the created order will ultimately succeed.

In the OT there are various names, titles, and descriptions of God. The most common are based on *El*, the Semitic name for God. The most important is the Hebrew word *Yahweh* which is often rendered as LORD in translations. This was the name by which God made himself known to Moses at the burning bush. The inner meaning of Yahweh is "I am who I am" or "I will be who I will be." In the NT "Lord" (*kyrios*) is used of Jesus.

In the NT, Jesus reveals the Fatherhood of God. While referring to God as Father, he claims the divine prerogative of forgiving sin, uses the divine title "I am" to refer to himself, and states that he and the Father are one. He is

revealed to be the eternal Word, one with the Father, true God made man. The church expresses this relationship of the Father, Son, and Holy Spirit in the doctrine of the Trinity.
Ex 3:14; Is 40:28-29; Jn 4:24; Acts 17:22f; Jn 27; Rom 8:17; Eph 1; Is 64:8.

Gospel. Good news from and about God. In the NT it is good news of the kingdom of God, of the arrival of God's Messiah, of the salvation achieved by the death and resurrection of Jesus. It is to be preached throughout the world in the power of the Holy Spirit.

The booklets we call "Gospels" are so called because they contain accounts of the gospel of God concerning Christ and the kingdom.
Is 40:9; 52:7; Mk 1:15; Mt 4:23; Rom 1:2 4; Rom 15:16,19; Gal 1:8f. See **Gospels,** sec. 1, and **Kingdom of God, Kingdom of heaven,** sec. 6.

Grace. In the OT God shows favor (grace) when he exercises compassion and mercy where strict justice would require punishment or no favor. Thus the Lord is said to deliver from oppression and distress and also to give prosperity and save life.

In the NT grace (*charis*) is a key theme word. Beneath it may be set that which God in Christ by the Spirit gives to undeserving sinners: regeneration, justification, salvation, forgiveness, and sanctification. Thus it stands in opposition to all religion that is attempting to please God by mere human endeavor.
Ps 4:2; 6:3; 9:14; 40:9; 41:5; 2 Kgs 13:23; 2 Sm 12:22; Rom 1:7; 6:14f; 1 Pt 5:10-12; Acts 15:11.

Heaven. In both the OT and the NT, "heaven" has a dual meaning: both the visible skies and the abode of God and of angels. The identification is not absolute, however. On the one hand, God preexists and indeed is creator of the "firmament" or "dome" of the heavens; on the other, both God and his messenger appear on, and are active in, the earth.

As Son of God, Jesus is said to have come from heaven in his Incarnation and to have returned there in his Ascension. United to him, believers are said to belong to heaven and thus to be pilgrims and sojourners on earth. From heaven Jesus will return to judge the world.
Dt 30:12f; Ps 2:4; Rv 11:13; 16:11; Acts 1:11; Eph 4:10; 2:6; 1 Cor 15:42f; Is 65:17; 66:22; 2 Pt 3:13.

Hell. The English word used to translate *Gehenna* (a valley for garbage outside Jerusalem) which Jewish writers from c. 200 B.C. had used to denote a place of punishment for the wicked. Jesus accepted this belief, refined it, and included it in his teaching. He warned people to escape the possibility of entering *Gehenna* by accepting the gospel of the kingdom and doing the will of God. In no way did Jesus make hell into a simple equivalent for the opposite of heaven. Other images used in the NT for hell apart from *Gehenna* are the place of weeping and gnashing of teeth, the torment of fire, and the place of perdition and ruin.

The descent of Jesus into Hades (the sphere of the departed) on holy Saturday may perhaps be understood as including a visit to hell.
Mt 5:22,29-30; 10:28; 18:9; 2 Kgs 23:10; Jas 3:6; Rv 9:1f; 11:7; 20:10.

Holy. God is holy; the essence of deity is holiness. He is the Holy One of Israel, whose very deity has the quality of being wholly other; thus he attracts his creation towards himself but it is not able to enter his near presence. By association with God, creatures and objects are classed as holy in a derivative sense. Thus the priesthood, the Temple, and its contents are holy, as is also the whole covenant people.

In the NT Jesus is the Holy One of God and the church is God's holy people because of their union with Jesus.

However, this holiness of union is also to be reflected in their character and way of life, which are to be without sin.
Am 4:2; Hos 11:9; 1 Sm 2:2; Is 6; Mk 1:24; Jn 6:69; Acts 3:14; 1 Pt 2:9; 1 Thes 4:5.

Hope. In order to live today for tomorrow, all people have a generalized form of hope, looking forward to this or that. As a Christian virtue, hope is produced by the Holy Spirit and is a looking forward to the future God has described in his revealed word. It is a humble and sure confidence that what God has promised he will bring to pass, for he is the Lord. The Christian is to abound in hope which is a sure and steadfast anchor for the soul. Such hope always exists alongside faith, for there must be trust in God and his word for there to be confidence about the future.
Eph 2:12; Rom 4:18; 15:13; Heb 6:19; 11:1; 1 Thes 1:3; 5:8; Gal 5:5-6; 1 Cor 13:13.

Judgment. As exercised by the tribal elder or king, judgment in the OT included the vindication of the righteous as well as the punishment of the wrongdoer. This was passed at the city gate or in the king's palace.

As exercised by the Lord as the God of the covenant with Israel, judgment is his defense and vindication of his people (especially of the poor, the widow, and the orphan); it may also include the chastisement or punishment of his people. In relation to the world, God is judge in the sense that he will judge all nations and people at the end of history and also in that he punishes those who maltreat Israel.

That there will be a "day of judgment" is clearly taught in the OT, but the teaching is in vivid imagery which is not easy to interpret. Further, there is a sense in which the whole world was judged when Christ was crucified at Calvary and in which anyone who rejects Christ and the gospel is judged by that unbelief.
Ex 18:13-16; 1 Kgs 7:7; 8:32; Is 9:6; Ps 72:1-2; Ps 7:7; 9:5; Ez 5:7-17; 7:3-9; Joel 4:9-21; Dn 7:9-11; Mt 10:15; 12:36; Jn 3:17-18; 12:48.

Justice, Justification. See **Righteousness,** sec. 6.

Kingdom of God, Kingdom of heaven. The central theme of the ministry of Jesus. His first public words were: "The time has come: the kingdom of God is close at hand." Jesus emphasized that God had become specially active in himself and through his ministry, making known and available his reign of salvation. Therefore a new type of life with a new relationship to God had become possible. This was because God had taken the initiative in sending his Messiah and making known the gospel. This new life came to those who responded to the gospel and entered the saving rule of God. This gracious reign of God was a kind of first installment of what would be in totality in the age to come. In John's Gospel the phrase "eternal life" is a dynamic equivalent to "kingdom of God" in Mark and Luke and "kingdom of heaven" in Matthew. "Heaven" is a synonym for "God."
Mt 3:2; 13; Mk 1:15; 4; 9:47; 1 Cor 15:24.

Last Things. See **Eschatology,** sec. 6.

Law. In the OT, it is the content of God's revelation made known through Moses to the tribes of Israel and recorded in the first five books of the OT. This governed Israel's entire conduct in its covenant relationship with God, from worship in the sanctuary to personal hygiene. Jesus, as the Messiah, came not to destroy but to fulfil the Law (bring it to completion in intention and meaning). He did this not only by his teaching but also in his sacrificial death.

The apostle Paul was very conscious that while the moral content of the Law was excellent, its effect upon people was to make them conscious of their failings and need of forgiveness. Thus he insisted that salvation could never be by "works of Law" but could only be by grace—a grace that expressed itself in acts of love for God's sake. James speaks of the "law of liberty."
Ps 19; Mt 5:17; Jn 1:17; 13:34; Rom 7:7-25; Jas 1:25; 2:8,12.

Life. God alone possesses life that is everlasting, immortal, and pure. As Creator he gives life to all his creatures, but it is a life that lasts only until physical death. This mortal life, however, ought to be truly good and satisfying when lived in faithful dependence upon God, the giver of life. Jesus taught that life need not be lost at death but through the gospel can be preserved, caught up, and transformed into resurrection life. In fact, eternal life begins within a person when he receives the gospel. This life is life with God in resurrection bodies of glory and immortality.
Mk 8:35; Jn 6:35; 11:25; 1 Cor 15:45.

Light. The symbolism of light functions in various ways but all are positive. God's holiness is "unapproachable light" and his self disclosure and revelation provide light for mind and heart, that is, truth and illumination. His word, uttered and spoken, is this light. Jesus is the Light of the world, for in him as incarnate Son and Messiah is everything that God is saying and offering to his creation. In a derivative sense his disciples are also the light of the world. He and they stand in contrast to the darkness (of ignorance, sin, and enmity towards God).
Ps 13:4; 119:105,130; Prv 29:13; Jn 1:9; 8:12; 1 Jn 1:7.

Lord. The Hebrew name of God, *Yahweh,* is often rendered in translations as Lord. In the Septuagint (the Greek translation of the OT) *Yahweh* becomes *kyrios.* And the first Christians who saw in Jesus God made man called him *kyrios.* Further, when Roman emperors insisted that they be worshipped as *kyrios,* the Christians refused. Thus "Jesus is Lord" was a basic, early Christian confession of faith.

The first day of the week, the day of the resurrection, became known as "the Lord's Day"; the Eucharist, instituted by Jesus at the Last Supper, is called "the Lord's Supper," and it has become traditional to call the "Our Father" prayer, "the Lord's Prayer."
Ex 3:14; Mt 22:43-45; 6:9-15; Lk 11:2-4; Acts 2:36; Rom

10:9; 1 Cor 8:5-6; 11:20; Phil 2:9,11; Rv 1:10; 17:14; 19:16.

Love. Though the Bible contains accounts of, and references to, the wide variety of types and forms of human love, its primary message is of the unique love of God himself for his creation, his faithful people, and his beloved Son (the Messiah). Its secondary message is of the love of human beings for each other after the pattern of God's love for them.

In the OT the love of the Lord for his covenant people in choosing and caring for them is a prominent theme in Deuteronomy. The prophet Hosea declared that God's love was like that of a faithful husband for his wife. Both insist that God himself is to be loved in response with the whole personality.

Jesus confirmed that the two great commandments are to love God and one's neighbor: he also insisted that his disciples are to love as he loved, including the enemy and the undesirable. Paul celebrates the love of God for sinners manifested in redemption through Christ and teaches that to love God in response is to fulfil the Law. John speaks of God's nature as that of love, the love of the Father and the Son, and insists that only those who love are the children of God.

Dt 4:37; 5:10; 6:5; 7:8; 10:12,15; 11:1; Lv 19:18; Hos 9:15; 11:1,14; Lk 10:25-37; Rm 8:35-39; 13:8-10; 1 Cor 13; Gal 5:13f; 1 Jn 4:17-21.

Man. Man is created in two sexes, giving rise to marriage, the family, tribe, and society. An essential part of God's creation, man is nevertheless a steward within creation with the duty of rightly ordering the world of nature. Further, man is created in order to enjoy fellowship with God: the possibility for this has been marred by the existence and power of sin. Thus the eternal Son of God, as Man, took human nature in order to redeem man and, breaking the power of sin, to restore man's fellowship with God. So

Christ is the Second Adam, and through him mortality is the gate into eternal and resurrection life. Man is to be thought of as an animated body rather than as a combination of soul and flesh.
Gn 1-3; Ps 8:5-6; 104:14-15; Rm 1:18-25; 5:12-17; 2 Cor 4:4; Col 1:15.

Mercy. The goodness of the heart from which love and kindness, compassion and faithfulness proceed. The Hebrew word *chesed* (mercy) is used both of the Lord and Israel. In the covenant, the Lord is merciful because, having chosen Israel, he is faithful and compassionate to his people. In turn the people, Israel, is to express *chesed* in loyalty and affection to the Lord.

In the NT, the Greek word *eleos* (mercy) is used both of God's will to save sinners and of the determination by believers to be compassionate and caring. In his identification with outcasts, Jesus showed mercy.
Ex 34:6; 1 Kgs 8:23; Jer 3:12f; Mt 9:13; Lk 10:37; 1 Pt 1:3; Tit 3:5.

Messiah. A Hebrew word meaning "the Anointed One" and rendered in the Greek form of "Christ" in the NT. In the OT "the Anointed One of God" was used of the reigning king, the priests, and of the future unique deliverer-king. Anointing referred to being anointed with oil when taking up office. In the time of Jesus, "Messiah" was often applied to a temporal king, a deliverer to set the Jews free from the yoke of Rome. Thus Jesus did not encourage this description of himself. However, his apostles declared that he was the long expected and true Messiah of Israel.
Ex 28:42; 1 Sm 9:16; 2 Sm 7:12-16; Ps 132:17; Jn 6:15; Mt 16:20; Acts 2:36.

Ministry. That which Jesus as Messiah and Lord exercises for the benefit of others, and also that which he shares with, entrusts to, and confers upon his followers for their mutual

service and in service of the world. Jesus is the origin, pattern, and enabler of ministry in the church. Each and every believer shares in this ministry and to each one is given some spiritual gift to exercise. Certain believers are called into positions of leadership, such as apostle, prophet, evangelist, elder, or teacher, and thus they add to their basic diaconal ministry a further specific ministry of the word.
Mt 20:28; 25:44; Acts 14:23; Rom 15:25; 12:7; 1 Cor 16:15; Eph 4:11.

Miracle. Strictly speaking, there is no word in the Bible for "miracle," but a group of words convey the idea of God, as Lord of creation and history, directing events for his own particular purposes. This is very obvious in the OT where the plagues of Egypt, the crossing of the Red Sea, the entry into Canaan through the dried-up Jordan, and many other events are seen as caused directly by God as part of his revelation to, and saving of, his elect people. Such events are to increase their faith and trust.

The miracles of Jesus, such as controlling nature and healing diseases, are the result of the direct presence and activity of God in his beloved Son, the Messiah. They represent the power of the kingdom (saving reign) of God operative in human lives, fulfilling prophecy, overcoming Satan, expressing divine compassion, and creating faith. They were never done merely to attract attention. The apostles also "in the name of the Lord" continued his ministry.

Both the OT and NT accept that extraordinary events were performed by opponents of Israel or of Christ but see no revelation in them, except of the power of Satan.
Ps 131:1; 135:6-12; Jos 3:5; 1 Kgs 19:14; 2 Kgs 20:11; Is 29:18; 35:4-5; Mt 11:2-6; 12:28; 9:36; 14:14; 15:32; 1 Cor 12:10.

Parousia. Greek for "coming" or "arrival" and used in the NT for the Second Coming of Jesus to earth. Jesus himself

often spoke of the future arrival of the Son of Man (a description of himself taken from Daniel 7) in glory with the holy angels in order to judge the world. This climax of history would be preceded by a variety of signs in the skies and on earth. Paul took up this theme and set out a rich and varied teaching on the Second Coming of Jesus to gather his elect, to raise the dead, to judge the people, to inaugurate the new age, and to fulfil God's purposes. Some in the early church expected the parousia in the very near future. They carried out missionary activity in the light of this expectation.
Dn 7:13f; Mt 16:27; 24:29-30; 25:31; 26:64; Acts 1:11; 1 Thes 4:13f; 2 Thes 2:7f; 2 Pt 3:10-12; Rv 3:11; 22:20.

Poverty. Both the OT and the NT use the concept of poverty in two related but different ways—the materially poor and the spiritually poor. When the Israelites entered Canaan and adopted the settled life, the division between rich and poor was often a problem. The law of Moses had made provision for protecting the rights of the poor and needy, and the prophets thundered God's disapproval of maltreatment of the poor. Yet poverty was part of the scene; Jesus expected that "the poor will be always with you." Paul organized a collection for the poor.

In certain psalms belonging to the period after the Babylonian Exile, the identification of the materially poor with the truly pious and devout begins. This was taken up by Jesus who insisted that the poor were admitted to God's kingdom. Being free of the distraction and temptations of wealth, they were more able to receive the gospel.
Ex 22:21-24; Ps 9:13,19; 25:16; 40:18; 69:13; Mt 5:3; Mk 14:5-7; Lk 6:20; 14:15; 16:19-31; Rom 15:26f.

Prayer. In the OT, those words, thoughts, and actions (e.g., temple sacrifices) offered to the Lord, the covenant God of Israel. Prayer is meaningful and possible because God has chosen Israel. It is response to him of a varied kind:

confession of sin, praise, thanksgiving, petition, intercession, commitment, or dedication. While prayer is especially appropriate in the Temple, it is also appropriate anywhere in the sacred land, especially in the home. After the Exile in Babylon, prayer in the synagogue became common; this developed in various ways up to the NT period and thus exercised an important influence over the prayers of Christian worship.

For Jesus, prayer to the Father was as natural as taking food. Not only did he provide an example of a life of prayer, he also taught his disciples how to pray, emphasizing the intimate relationship with God as "Our Father," and praying for the good of one's enemies. In the Acts, the early church is portrayed as a community of prayer, addressing Jesus directly and also praying to the Father in his name. Paul's epistles contain many prayers and calls to pray, along with teaching on the role of the Spirit in individual prayer. The Epistle to the Hebrews sets forth the role of Jesus, exalted priest, in prayer.
1 Sm 1:10ff; 1 Kgs 3:6-9; 8:23-53; 2 Mc 15:22-24; Mt 6:6-8; Mk 12:40; Lk 6:12; Jn 17; Rom 8:26ff; Heb 4:14-16.

Preaching. Proclaiming and announcing God's word to people as his herald. In the OT, the prophets announced God's word of judgment and salvation, comfort and condemnation. In the NT, John the Baptist proclaimed the arrival of God's kingly reign and his Messiah; Jesus proclaimed the arrival of this kingdom in his ministry; the apostles, evangelists, and traveling teachers of the early church announced that through the death and resurrection of Jesus, God's salvation was freely offered to all who repented of their sins and believed this good news.
Mk 1:4; 1:38; Mt 10:27; 24:14; Acts 28:31; Rm 10:14; 2 Cor 4:5. See **Gospel,** sec. 6.

Predestination. See **Election,** sec. 6.

Providence. The confident and humble conviction that God, as the creator and sustainer of the universe, rules all natural forces and historical events according to his own will and directs them to his own appointed goal. The OT and NT teach that God is in charge and that nothing happens without his being involved directly or indirectly. Not being a philosophical textbook, the Bible does not attempt to answer problems of human free will and divine sovereignty: rather believers are encouraged to trust in God always because of who he is and what he has done.
Ps 147:8f; Mt 10:29; Ps 2:4; Prv 21:1; Ezr 6:22; Dt 28:15ff; Rom 8:35ff.

Reconciliation. The hostility between mankind and God because of sin and evil was removed by the sacrificial death of Jesus, the Christ, at Calvary. On behalf of the human race, Jesus, as representative and substitute, made an act of atonement which objectively removed the barrier of sin and the hostility which prevented God and his creatures being friends. In the gospel, preached by the church, reconciliation is offered by God to his enemies; and by their receiving of the gospel they become his reconciled children and thus his friends.
Rom 5:10-21; 2 Cor 5:18-19; Eph 2:11-22; Col 1:19-20.

Redemption. In everyday life, the freedom secured by the payment of an appropriate price. Used as a metaphor in both OT and NT of God's saving activity and its liberating results. God is thus the redeemer of Israel as a people and of particular individual Israelites when he saves them from calamity, distress, or disaster. In Christ, God secures redemption—freedom from the power of sin and final salvation—for believers. The metaphor suggests that Christ makes a payment to God on behalf of sinners for their liberation and salvation.
Ps 44:27; 78:42; 119:134; Dt 7:8; 13:6; 15:15; Mk 10:45; Rm 3:24; Eph 1:7; Col 1:14; Ti 2:14; Heb 9:15.

Regeneration. The entry of God's Spirit and the gift of eternal life into the believer's heart so that he is a temple of the Holy Spirit. This is intimately associated with the hearing and believing of the gospel and the act of baptism. It is a being spiritually begotten by God in order to call him Father. Also used of the act of renewal at the end of the age when God will make the "new heavens and new earth."
Mt 19:28; Jn 1:13; 3:3-8; 1 Jn 2:29; 4:7; 1 Pt 1:3; 1:23; 2:2; Ti 3:5.

Repentance. Used of both God and human beings when they change their attitudes. In his covenant relation with Israel, God acted as in a personal relationship. Thus he sometimes changed his mind as to his intended blessing upon or judgment of his people. As used of sinful human beings, repentance implies that they are turning to God in creaturely dependance and away from what is offensive to him. Thus not only is there a change of mind and direction but also remorse for offending God and commitment to him. In the NT, Jesus and the apostles insisted that the right response to the gospel was repentance with faith.
Dt 30:1-10; Am 7:3,6; 4:6-11; Hos 6:1-3; Mk 1:15; Lk 15:11-24; Acts 2:38; 3:19.

Resurrection. Either resuscitation to the former mortal life or raising from death in a new immortal body into everlasting life. The Christian gospel and hope centers on the second. Elijah, Elisha, and Jesus raised dead people to continue their mortal life and to die again. However, in the latter part of the OT, the belief begins to emerge that at the end of this age the dead will be raised for life in the new kingdom of God. The Pharisees held to such teaching. The resurrection of Jesus on the third day in an immortal body of glory and his exaltation into heaven in that body gave to the first Christians the very core and center of their own faith and their message to the world. Because Christ has risen, God's salvation is available to the world and this includes for

each believer a body like that of Christ for his life in the age to come. There is no Christian message unless Christ rose from death in a new, glorious, immortal body.
1 Kgs 17:17-24; 2 Kgs 4:18-37; Dn 12:2; 2 Mc 7:9,11,23; Mt 9:18-26; Jn 11: 1-44; 20-21; Rm 4:24; 1 Cor 15.

Revelation. The Scriptures are the record of God's self-disclosure and thus, as used by the Holy Spirit, become the channel of revelation today. The OT is a record of the disclosure by God of himself and his will as the Lord of history and of nature. His activity as Creator and Lord of history is made clear through the words he gives to chosen individuals: to Moses, the prophets, and "the wise." Precisely how God spoke to them and in them is a complex question, but the result of what they heard was written down and became, eventually, the Old Testament. God is chiefly and fully revealed in Jesus: to see and hear him was to receive revelation from the Father. In his ministry of word and works, and chiefly by his passion and resurrection, he both provided the fullest disclosure of God—his character, purposes, and will—and brought salvation to mankind. The Spirit who filled Jesus also came upon his apostles so that they might know his mind and will and do what he wanted done. Their teaching was therefore inspired by him and was further disclosure of God's grace. As written this became the New Testament.
Ex 33:11; Is 6; Prv 1:7; Mt 11:25-27; Gal 1:12,16; Heb 1:1.

Righteousness. Used in several ways: of a state of innocence, of being in the right before the Law, and of being placed in the right by God. The basic meaning in the OT is to be sought within the legal processes and is the justice required by the Law. The Law itself is righteous and calls for righteousness. At court the judge or king declares that some are righteous (in the right) before the Law. Thus the ideal king (Messiah) will embody justice and be righteous.

When used of God by the OT writers (especially in Is

40-66), righteousness points to God's right actions on behalf of Israel, that is, his saving power and will exercised on their behalf. Therefore, when Paul presents God's righteousness as his action in declaring sinners to be in a right relationship with himself because of the merit and righteousness of Christ, he is developing an OT theme. Having received the gift of righteousness, sinners are justified in God's sight because justice has been accounted to them. Then, in the power of the Holy Spirit, justified sinners are to be righteous in real terms day by day.
Ex 23:7f Dt 25:1; Prv 17:15,26; Ps 119:7; 72:1-2; Is 9:6; 51:1; Mal 3:18; Is 45:24; Dn 9:16; Rom 3-8; Gal.

Sabbath. The seventh day of the week in the Israelite calendar: a regular holy day with obligatory rest from normal work. Its observance was required by the law of Moses and, during the centuries immediately before Christ, this became a distinctive mark of Judaism. How to observe it was much discussed by the rabbis. Jesus observed the Sabbath in what he saw as its original purpose—"The Sabbath was made for man and not man for the Sabbath." Since the early church kept the Lord's Day, only its Jewish membership kept the Sabbath. In Christian theology, the Sabbath came to refer to the future life of the kingdom of God.
Gn 2:1-3; Ex 20:8-10; Lv 16:31; 23:1-3; Dt 5:12-15; Mk 2:27; Heb 4.

Salvation. The God of the Bible is preeminently the Lord who saves; he is the God of salvation. What his salvation includes and means grows in scope and clarity from the OT to the NT. It can mean victory in battle (saved from enemies and defeat), recovery from illness, and intervention on behalf of the poor and needy, all in the context of the election of Israel as his covenant people. In the later part of the OT (e.g., Is 40-66), salvation begins to mean a new Israel, new Zion, new world, and new revelation from the Lord. And this is connected with the growing hope for the ideal king of righteousness (Messiah), the agent of God's salvation.

The NT emphasizes many times that salvation is from God and is centered on Jesus, the Messiah. It may include physical healing, but it always includes forgiveness of sins, union with the Lord Jesus, and the promise of being a part of the new people with new bodies in God's new world of the age to come. Thus salvation is what God has done in Christ, what he is doing now in the work of the Holy Spirit, and what he will do at and after the Last Judgment. There will be complete victory for his will over all sin and evil, and people will be liberated into the perfect enjoyment of his presence and blessings.

Jgs 2:16; 8:22; 12:3; Ps 18:47; 24:5; 25:5; Is 62:1; Mt 1:21; 19:25; 24:22, Lk 1:77; Rm 13:11; Ti 3:5; 1 Pt 2:2.

Satan. The devil, an angel disobedient to God and opposed to his plan of salvation for mankind. The NT teaching represents not only a development of OT insights but also the adoption of doctrine from Jewish intertestamental (apocryphal) literature. As described in Job, Satan is a member of the heavenly host who acts as the accuser in order to test the reactions of men. However, in the later apocryphal teaching, Satan (Gk. *diabolos,* "accuser") has become the one who actually inflicts evil; he is the prince of evil spirits who has been expelled from heaven by the archangel Michael.

Jesus saw himself in open conflict with Satan and believed that as Messiah he had to overcome him. By his death and resurrection he struck a deadly blow, but Satan is still active until his judgment at the end of the age. Part of the Christian life is to resist Satan.

Jb 1:6ff; 2:1ff; Zc 3:1-2; Lk 4:1-13; 22:53; Mt 12:26; 1 Pt 5:8; Eph 4:27; Rv 12:12; 20:7.

Sin. That deviation and distortion in human beings which is offensive to God and prevents true fellowship with him. In the OT a cluster of words convey the character of sin as deliberate and willful action contrary to God's known will expressed in his Law. Sin is thus found in individuals, tribes, and nations. As to the origins of sin, there is the Genesis story of Adam and Eve who desired to have what was not theirs and thereby broke their relationship with God in the act of disobedience. Not only do the prophets declare God's judgment upon sin, but the Law of Moses made provision for atonement for sin by a repentant Israel.

In the NT the presence and power of sin in human lives is presented as that which causes mankind to need salvation. Sin is a state of heart or mind and even an evil power within mankind which has to be conquered and eliminated by the Messiah. Jesus is the friend of sinners. In the future age of the kingdom, there will be no sin; but sin will remain as part of the present world and age until the Last Judgment. Christians are called to overcome sin in their hearts and not to commit sin in practice.
Gn 3; Ps 38; 51; Mt 9:10; 11:19; Lk 15:7,10; Rm 1:18-32; 5:12; Jas 1:14-15; 1 Jn 3:4,8; 5:17.

Spirit. The human spirit is that invisible breath which is the source of life. The spirit of God is the invisible power of God active in the world and in individuals. The latter develops through the OT into the full doctrine of the Holy Spirit in the baptismal formula of Mt 28:19. This development is by no means straightforward and easy to follow. In the OT the Spirit of God is said to inspire prophets, to create charismatic leaders (judges), to deliver people from disasters, to pervade the created order, and to cause extraordinary phenomena.

In the NT the Holy Spirit is in conflict with evil spirits, and it is because he is anointed, guided, and filled by the Holy Spirit that Jesus, as Messiah, is able to cast out evil spirits and be God's faithful servant. The selfsame Spirit who inhabits the resurrected Jesus also fills his body, the church, to baptize his disciples and to indwell their hearts, assisting them to overcome evil and to do the will of the Lord.
Gn 6:17; 7:15,22; Nm 11:17ff; Jgs 3:10; 11:29; 1 Kgs 18:12;

2 Kgs 3:16; Ps 78:39; Is 31:3; Mt 3:11-17; Lk 4:1,14; Jn 14:16-17; 15:26; 16:7-14; Acts 1:8; 2:1ff; Rom 8.

Suffering. The experience of pain of mind or body which God allows, uses, and even sends in this present evil age, but which he will wholly remove from the coming age of the kingdom of God. Suffering as the result of personal sin is expressed through conflict, pain, corruption, drudgery, and death. Suffering as a divine chastisement or punishment can take a variety of forms from illness to disaster. Even the righteous do not escape suffering because living in a sinful world, they attract the power of evil. It is thus to be expected that the servant of the Lord described by Isaiah, and fulfilled by Jesus, the Messiah, should be known as the suffering servant (Is 53). Jesus had to suffer in order to become a ransom and sacrifice for sin. Further, his disciples are called to share his suffering.
Gn 3:15-19; Is 65:17ff; Hos 8:7; Am 1-2; Lk 13:1-5; 1 Pt 1:10-12; Rom 8:28-29; Rv 21:4.

Temptation, Testing. In God's providence people are put to the test; temptation is to make trial of a person. Both the OT and NT teach that God himself places his children in situations which reveal the quality of their faith or commitment: the purpose is to strengthen. They further indicate that God allows Satan (within limits) to test his children in order to keep them watchful and alert. Jesus himself was tempted by Satan and (simultaneously) tested by God. Temptation is not sin; it becomes sin when yielded to. How this happens is well illustrated in Gn 3:1-19. Resistance is followed by hesitation and weakening before surrender to the temptation.
Gn 22:1; Ex 16:4; Jb 1:12; 2:6; Mt 4:1-11; Lk 22:28; Acts 20:19; 1 Cor 10:13; Heb 4:15; Jas 1:2ff; 1 Pt 5:10.

Ten Commandments (The Ten Words). Spoken by the heavenly voice from Mount Sinai in the hearing of the tribes of Israel and afterwards twice written down "by the finger of

God" on both sides of two tablets of stone. The first pair were shattered by Moses because of Israel's sin and the second pair were deposited inside the Ark of the covenant. They represent the essence of the covenant between the Lord and the Israelites of which Moses was the mediator. Thus they set forth the character of God and the required response to his saving activity on Israel's behalf.
Ex 19:16-20:17; 25:16; 31:18; 32:15-16,19; 34:1,28; 40:20; Dt 5:6-21.

Word of God. In OT times the spoken word was held to have a particular dynamic quality, especially in the utterance of solemn words in covenants, curses, promises, and blessings. Thus the "word of God" as the source of the created order, the origin of the call to service, and the content of the prophetic message was a word that achieved its purpose. Further, when written down it held its dynamic power.

In the NT the "word of God" is variously used of the gospel—the good news of the kingdom—by Paul and in the Acts; however, in John's writings the "Word" is the Son himself who also speaks the "word of the Father." The word has inherent power for it is always accompanied by the power and presence of the Holy Spirit.
Gn 1:3; 12:1; Dt 4:13; 10:4; 32:47; Is 9:8; 55:10-11; Lk 5:1; 8:11; Jn 1:1-14; 8:55; 14:24; 17:6; Acts 4:4,29-31; 6:4; 8:4; 1 Cor 14:36; 2 Cor 2:17; 6:7.

World. Sometimes used in a neutral sense of either the universe as created order or of the world of human beings. However, most often in the NT it refers to the human race in a state of rebellion against its Creator, in the grip of the evil one (Satan), and dominated by its pride and covetousness. It is people impregnated by sinfulness. Christ comes into this world, but he comes without sin in order to overcome and deal with that which has made the human race into a sinful and rebellious people. Thus he offers himself as propitiation or expiation for the sins of the whole world and sends the

Holy Spirit to convince the world of its sin. His disciples are to be wholly involved *in* this world but not to be *of* this world. At the end of the age, this world will be redeemed, regenerated, and renewed.
Mt 4:8-9; 5:14; 16:26; Jn 1:10; 16:11,21; 1 Cor 1:21; 1 Jn 2:2; 4:14; 5:19; Rv 11:15.

Index